CW01096170

About this Learning Guide

Shmoop Will Make You a Better Lover*
*of Literature, History, Poetry, Life...

Our lively learning guides are written by experts and educators who want to show your brain a good time. Shmoop writers come primarily from Ph.D. programs at top universities, including Stanford, Harvard, and UC Berkeley.

Want more Shmoop? We cover literature, poetry, bestsellers, music, US history, civics, biographies (and the list keeps growing). Drop by our website to see the latest.

www.shmoop.com

Table of Contents

Introduction

In a Nutshell

The Two Gentlemen of Verona is a comedy about the adventures of two bosom buddies, Valentine and Proteus. When Proteus falls in love with his best friend's girlfriend, the guys find themselves torn between the bonds of male friendship and romance. (If you're thinking all this sounds like a modern day "bromantic comedy," you're right. *Two Gentlemen of Verona* is the great, great grandfather of buddy flicks like the 2009 comedy *I Love You Man*.)

Written as early as 1590-91, *Two Gentlemen* appears to be William Shakespeare's first play. (As usual, some literary critics are divided over this issue, but we're going with the editors of *The Norton Shakespeare* and the editors of *The Oxford Shakespeare* on this one.) As Shakespeare's first theatrical effort, *Two Gentlemen* has been referred to as a "limping forerunner" of Shakespeare's later works. Even famous literary scholar Harold Bloom says it's "the weakest of all Shakespeare's comedies." We, on the other hand, prefer to think of *Two Gentlemen* as Shakespeare's test kitchen, where a budding young playwright begins to work out the recipe for his "comedies" and begins to explore themes and conventions that he'll develop more fully in later works – particularly the themes of male friendship and heterosexual love, which come into conflict in plays like *The Merchant of Venice* and also in Shakespeare's collection of *Sonnets*.

Like all test kitchen creations, *Two Gentlemen* is far from perfect – there are multiple plot inconsistencies and many scenes feature only a couple of speakers at a time. On this latter point, Jean Howard notes that it's "as if Shakespeare had not yet mastered the skill of orchestrating a full complement of stage voices and bodies." The play is also notable for its controversial and somewhat bizarre ending. We don't want to spoil it for you, but be sure to check out "What's Up With the Ending?" for all of our thoughts on it.

Two Gentlemen of Verona is one of the least frequently staged Shakespeare plays, but it also happens to have inspired one of the greatest film adaptations of all time – the 1998 film *Shakespeare in Love*, co-written by Tom Stoppard (the guy responsible for *Rosencrantz and Guildenstern Are Dead*). *Shakespeare in Love* is a fictional account of how young Will Shakespeare overcomes writer's block to pen *Romeo and Juliet*. The film references several of Shakespeare's works but borrows most heavily from *Two Gentlemen*, including several speeches (like Valentine's famous "What light is light" monologue) and scenes (like Lance's "bit with the dog").

Shakespeare's main source for *Two Gentlemen* is Jorge de Montemayor's *Diana Enamorada*. (It was published in English 1598 but Shakespeare may have read an earlier version in French.) Shakespeare's play is also influenced by Thomas Elyot's *The Book Named the Governor*

(1531), especially the story of Titus and Gisippus (Gisippus gives his best friend, Titus, the woman he is supposed to marry after Titus falls in love with her in Book 2, Chapter 12).

Why Should I Care?

Earlier, we said that reading *Two Gentlemen* is like getting a glimpse of Shakespeare's test kitchen – you know, the place where he works out his "recipe" for his later comedies. If this isn't enough to make you want to check out *Two Gentlemen of Verona*, then try to think of it this way: Most people have felt torn between a romantic relationship and loyalty to friends at some point in their lives. Maybe you've had to decide between, say, joining your pals for a night of bowling & pizza or a romantic date with the person you've been crushing on since the fourth grade. And we all know someone who has betrayed a best friend by stealing (or trying to steal) his/her prom date, right? It's not very nice but it's the stuff literature, poetry, and music lyrics have been made of for as long as anyone can remember – whether it's the *Twilight* series love triangle between Bella, Edward, and Jacob, or famous song lyrics like "My Best Friend's Girl" (1978) by The Cars. *Two Gentlemen of Verona* is all about messy relationships between friends and lovers.

But the thing to remember about *Two Gentlemen* is that, in Shakespeare's day, male friendship was often valued above all other relationships, especially heterosexual romance. Marriage was pretty important too, but male bonds trumped *everything*. This is partly due to sixteenth- and seventeenth-century attitudes about gender. For many writers and philosophers, women weren't considered to be capable of true friendship. Ever read the famous essay "Of Friendship," by Montaigne? Check out what Montaigne has to say about women: "Moreover, to say truth, the ordinary talent of women is not such as is sufficient to maintain the conference and communication required to the support of this sacred tie; nor do they appear to be endued with constancy of mind, to sustain the pinch of so hard and durable a knot." Yikes!

Our point is this: Shakespeare's play is about love triangles and whether or not our friends deserve our loyalty more than our romantic partners. If you think about it, *The Two Gentlemen of Verona* isn't so different from some popular "bromantic comedies" like *Knocked Up* and *I Love You Man*.

Book Summary

When the play opens, Valentine and Proteus (a.k.a. the two gentlemen of Verona) are in the middle of an emotional goodbye. You see, Valentine is leaving for Milan and his BFF is sad to

see him go. Proteus would join him on his adventure, but he's in love with Julia so he's decided to stay home in Verona to be with her.

Meanwhile, Julia is hanging out with her woman in waiting, Lucetta. The two discuss which one of popular Julia's suitors is the dreamiest. Julia is partial to Proteus, but he's the only guy who *hasn't* proposed to her yet. As Julia wonders why that is, Lucetta whips out a letter from Proteus and hands it over to Julia, who pretends she's too modest to read it. After a silly little game of "I don't want to read it, send it back," Julia demands the love note and then tears it to shreds when Lucetta teases her. She immediately regrets it and tries to piece it back together.

Meanwhile, when Proteus's dad hears that people have been talking trash about him for not sending his son to travel abroad (that's what all the noblemen do, apparently), he decides to send Proteus to Milan, where he can become a well-rounded person (by going to jousts and hanging out with the children of other noblemen). Proteus tries to waffle – he was hoping to spend his summer going to the beach and hanging out at Dairy Queen with his girl Julia, but his dad won't let him wriggle out of traveling abroad. Proteus visits Julia one last time – they exchange rings and she cries. Then Proteus heads to Milan, where Valentine has been hanging out.

Speaking of Valentine…in Milan, he has met and fallen in love with the beautiful and sassy Silvia. Silvia treats Valentine like her "servant" and Valentine loves every minute of it. (That's how guys and girls flirt in "courtly romance" literature, which Shakespeare is, to some extent, making fun of here.)

When Proteus shows up, he promptly falls in love with Silvia, forgetting all about the girl he left back home. Then Proteus does something awful – he tattles on Valentine (who plans to elope with Silvia) to Silvia's protective father, the Duke of Milan. When the Duke approaches Valentine, a steamy lover letter to Silvia and a rope ladder fall out of the young man's jacket. (We're not sure how all that stuff fit in his coat.) The Duke says something like "Aha! You're planning to climb that ladder up to my daughter's bedroom. Get out of my sight." Ultimately, the Duke banishes Valentine from Milan – if Valentine shows his face in town ever again, he'll be put to death.

Meanwhile, back in Verona, Julia has decided she's going to travel to Milan to find her beloved Proteus. She dresses like a boy so she can travel without being accosted by any "lascivious men" who would try to ravish her. Julia gets gussied up in a pair of "breeches" (pants) and a fancy codpiece (what amounts to a decorative jockstrap) and heads to Milan, where she discovers her beloved Proteus…hitting on Silvia.

While this is happening, our boy Valentine is riding through a forest somewhere between Milan and Mantua when a band of outlaws pounce on him. Valentine lies about having killed a man and the outlaws are totally impressed. They decide he should be the Robin Hood to their band of merry thieves, so they invite him to be the leader of their forest dwelling gang. Valentine

agrees to live with them in the forest but makes them promise not to hurt any "silly women" or helpless travelers.

Back in Milan, Julia is calling herself "Sebastian" and has landed a job as Proteus's errand boy. (Apparently, Julia wants to size up the competition in secret.) When Proteus sends "Sebastian" to deliver a ring to Silvia, "Sebastian" and Silvia get to talking. Silvia refuses to take the ring because she knows it once belonged to Julia. Julia admits to the audience that this is a good thing because she would have "scratched out" Silvia's eyes if she wasn't such a nice person.

Silvia is still in love with banished Valentine, so she convinces her good friend Eglamour to help her find him – the two run off to the forest, where Silvia is kidnapped by the outlaws, who proceed to take her to their leader, Valentine. (How convenient.) Meanwhile, the Duke has learned his daughter ran away and has organized a posse to track her down in the forest. Proteus tags along.

In the forest, Proteus catches up to Silvia and "rescues" her from the outlaws. He then tries to convince her that she should drop Valentine and get with him. When she refuses to love him, he tries to rape her. Before Proteus can assault Silvia, however, Valentine steps in and…yells at Proteus for betraying their friendship. (Yeah, we were sort of hoping Proteus would be punished for trying to rape Silvia, but no such luck.)

Proteus says he's sorry for being a lousy friend and Valentine says, "All that was mine in Silvia I give thee" (5.4). There are a few ways to read this but you'll have to go to "What's Up with the Ending?" if you want to know what *we* think…

Before Proteus can respond, "Sebastian" faints dramatically and then reveals that "he" is actually Julia. Proteus takes one look at his former girlfriend and falls back in love with her. Julia forgives Proteus and the two are engaged. The Duke, who has also arrived in the forest, decides that Valentine is a great guy after all, so he gives his daughter to him as a "gift." Valentine thinks this is just swell. (Apparently, Silvia does too, but we don't hear a peep out of her after Proteus's attempted rape.) Valentine suggests a double wedding is in order and the crew heads back to the Duke's place for a big reception.

Act 1, Scene 1

- Welcome to Verona…at least we think we're in Verona. The only indication Shakespeare gives us about the location is in the play's title.
- Two BFFs, Valentine and Proteus, are in the middle of a long and emotional goodbye. You see, Valentine is embarking on an adventure so he might learn a thing or two about "the wonders of the world abroad." (By "world abroad," he means the world outside of Verona.)
- Valentine wishes his dear friend would throw some jeans and sneakers into a backpack and join him (as opposed to "living dully sluggarized at home"), but since Proteus is in love with a girl in Verona, he understands why Proteus wants to stay behind.

- In between bouts of dramatic sighing, Proteus begs Valentine to think of him while he's on his adventure and promises to pray for Valentine while he's away.
- Then Valentine makes a snide remark and implies that Proteus's love for the yet-to-be-named mystery girl is "shallow." To emphasize his point that he doesn't like his buddy's romance, he compares Proteus to "Leander," a mythical/literary figure who drowned while swimming across the Hellespont to see his girlfriend, "Hero." (The Hellespont, by the way, is one of the Turkish straits – it's got a nasty reputation for drowning swimmers.)
- Cynical Valentine continues to berate his pal for loving a woman and insists that love turns men into slaves and fools. (Geez – this guy's almost as bad as Mercutio in *Romeo and Juliet*.)
- Finally, Valentine says he's got to run or else he'll miss his boat to Milan. (Yeah. We know that Verona and Milan are totally landlocked but Shakespeare obviously doesn't care, so let's just go with it.)
- Valentine and Proteus finally say goodbye and promise to write.
- Proteus is left alone on stage. He whines that his love for Julia (we now have a name for our mystery girl) has caused him to neglect his homework assignments, causes him to argue with his friends, and causes him to generally waste his time moping around. (Kind of like Shakespeare's other lovelorn character, Romeo, when he crushes on Rosaline, or Duke Orsino in *Twelfth Night*.)
- Then "Speed" shows up. (Speed is Valentine's clownish servant.)
- Speed wants to know if Proteus has seen his master.
- Proteus brings Speed up to speed on Valentine's recent departure and then the two engage in a silly conversation that involves one guy insulting the other guy by punning on the word "sheep." The dialogue's a little complicated, but it basically boils down to "You're a sheep." "No I'm not – you're a sheep." (You can listen to the witty exchange here, compliments of Audible.com.)
- Proteus wants to know if Speed delivered his love letter to the luscious Julia and then Speed tells a dirty joke that involves, you guessed it, sheep.
- After an amusing and slightly exasperating comic routine, Speed shakes down Proteus for some money and finally says that, yes, he delivered Proteus's letter to Julia.
- Proteus is bummed to hear that Julia didn't get all excited when Speed delivered the letter and he reasons that she must have been put off by the annoying messenger (that would be Speed).
- Proteus decides he'll find a new messenger to deliver his love notes to Julia.

Act 1, Scene 2

- Meanwhile, Julia is lounging around her garden having a little girl talk with her woman in waiting, Lucetta.
- Julia is in desperate need of some advice about the following: Should she fall in love? If so,

which one of her dozens of suitors should she hook up with?

- Julia ticks off a few names of guys who are drooling over her before she gets around to asking Lucetta what she thinks of Proteus.
- Lucetta's first response is something like "That clown?", but then she catches herself and says what Julia wants to hear – that Proteus is the best of the lot. Plus, he seems to love Julia the most.
- Julia wonders why Proteus hasn't proposed to her yet and declares that you can measure a guy's love by the amount of time he spends *telling* you he loves you. According to Julia, Proteus hasn't spent nearly enough time doing this.
- Then Lucetta is all, "Oh yeah, this letter from Proteus came for you earlier" and gives Julia the love letter. (Yeah, yeah. We thought Speed gave the letter directly to Julia too. Speed may have lied to Proteus. Or this just may be a slip up on Shakespeare's part – either way, Julia now has the letter.)
- Julia orders Lucetta to return the letter to Proteus, but then she immediately regrets it. She gets mad at Lucetta – apparently, Lucetta should have known that Julia would be too modest to read a letter from a boy.
- Then Julia, who is beginning to sound pretty silly, comes to her senses and admits that *she's* the one with the problem. She pretended to be mad that Proteus sent her a letter when deep down inside she was jumping for joy.
- Julia calls back Lucetta, who returns and then plays "keep away" with the letter and teases Julia about Proteus.
- Julia, who is now back in tantrum mode, grabs the letter and tears it to shreds to demonstrate that she doesn't really care about love.
- Julia's roller coaster ride of emotions isn't over – she immediately bends down and gathers the bits and pieces of the letter.
- She reads each snippet of paper aloud and tries to piece the fragments together. (It ends up sounding like the kind of poetry you make by randomly putting together word magnets on the refrigerator.)
- Then Julia's dad calls her to the dinner table and she runs off for a slice of pizza.

Act 1, Scene 3

- At his house in Verona, Antonio (Proteus's dad) learns that his brother has been talking smack about him for not sending Proteus to travel abroad like all the other noblemen's kids. (By "kids," we mean "sons," because noblemen didn't let their daughters go globetrotting.)
- Antonio thinks that his brother is right – if Proteus doesn't explore the world now while he's young, he'll regret it when he's an old man. Plus, a young man's education isn't complete without a little travel.
- After some deliberation, Antonio and Panthino decide Proteus should be sent to the Emperor's court, where he'll get to hang out at jousts and learn how to schmooze with all

the other noblemen's kids.

- (OK. We're just going to say this now to avoid any confusion about the plot later on. Even though Antonio says he's going to send Proteus to the *Emperor's* court, Proteus ends up at the *Duke's* court. Again, we forgive Big Willy for the minor inconsistency.)
- It just so happens that a group of friends are travelling to the "Emperor's" court tomorrow so Proteus can tag along.
- Then Proteus enters the room but he doesn't see his dad and Panthino. Proteus whips out a love letter from Julia and proceeds to say things like "Sweet love, sweet lines, sweet life!"
- Antonio interrupts Proteus slobbering all over the note and says, "Whatcha reading?"
- Proteus lies and says it's a letter from Antonio. "Oh goodie," says his dad, "let *me* read it then."
- Antonio announces that he's got great news for his son – Proteus is going to the "Emperor's" court, where he'll get to hang out with his BFF, Antonio!
- Proteus tries to find an excuse to stay in Verona but his dad insists that he leave tomorrow.
- Proteus is left alone on stage to complain – he says he wishes he had just told his father the truth about the love letter from Julia.

Act 2, Scene 1

- Back in Milan, Speed helps Proteus put on his gloves and finds a third glove that belongs to Silvia – the girl with whom Valentine has recently fallen head over heels in love.
- Speed teases Valentine about his crush and says that Valentine's been moping around like a lovesick puppy: sighing, folding his arms, singing love songs, refusing to eat, and crying like a girl weeping over her dead grandmother (he seriously says that).
- Then Speed proceeds to insult Valentine and Silvia by implying that Silvia is ugly but Valentine thinks she's beautiful because he's wearing love goggles.
- Silvia enters and lovelorn Valentine proceeds to shower her with compliments.
- Silvia refers to Valentine as her "servant" and then proceeds to treat him like one.
- Brain Snack: We see this kind of thing all the time in "courtly love" literature (like Chaucer's *Troilus and Criseyde*, c. 1350), where guys devote themselves to their lady-loves and call themselves "servants." Shakespeare is sort of poking fun of Valentine *and* the whole courtly love convention here, even as he participates in it.
- We find out that Silvia has recently asked Valentine to write a love letter to an unnamed "friend" of Silvia's. Valentine, who doesn't understand that Silvia really meant she wanted him to write a love letter to *her*, hands over the note and is all "I hope your friend likes it. It's not very good because I don't know anything about the person I was writing to."
- Silvia is peeved at the generic contents of the letter and shoves it back at Valentine, telling him to try again – this time, the letter should be more passionate.
- Poor Valentine is baffled by Silvia's behavior until Speed explains why Silvia is so upset.
- Speed announces it's dinner time and Valentine says something like "I'm not hungry. I've already dined on love."

Act 2, Scene 2

- Back in Verona, Julia and Proteus say a teary goodbye before Proteus departs on his trip.
- After Julia begs Proteus to be faithful to her, the couple exchange rings and "seal the bargain with a holy kiss."
- Proteus makes a weird speech about how he's going to be true – but *if*, by some odd chance he's *not* faithful to Julia, he won't be able to forgive himself. (Gee. We wonder what will happen when Proteus goes to Milan…)
- Julia runs off without saying another word.
- Panthino arrives to fetch Proteus – it's time to ship out.

Act 2, Scene 3

- Lance (Proteus's servant) and Crab (Lance's dog) enter the stage and Lance makes a big speech to the audience about how he must accompany Proteus to the "Emperor's" court in Milan. Lance's entire family is upset that Lance is leaving – his mom's "weeping," his dad's "wailing," his sister's "crying," the maid "howling," etc. The only member of the family that couldn't care less is Lance's beloved dog, Crab.
- To demonstrate his dog's indifference, Lance takes off his shoes and then proceeds to use his foot-ware, a staff (walking stick), and a hat as props to reenact what went down at his family home when he broke the sad news of his imminent departure.
- Panthino enters, interrupting Lance's little skit, and orders Lance aboard the ship that's setting sail for Milan. (Again, we know Verona and Milan are landlocked, but Shakespeare *really* likes to incorporate sea voyages into his plays – he even managed to sneak one into *Hamlet*.)
- Lance can hardly speak because he's sobbing about his cruel, unloving dog, who isn't even sad to see him go.
- One dirty joke and some silly banter later, Panthino finally convinces Lance to board the ship to avoid losing his job as Proteus's servant.

Act 2, Scene 4

- At the Duke's court in Milan, Silvia and Valentine are busy flirting like two "courtly lovers" (remember what we said about their little game of master and servant back in Act 2, Scene 1)? Meanwhile, a guy named Thurio sneers at the happy twosome.
- Speed notices that Thurio is jealous, so he does what all of Shakespeare's clownish

servants do best – he starts trouble. Before we know it, Thurio and Valentine are insulting each other.

- At one point, Silvia chimes in that Thurio's face is turning red but, finally, she tires of the silly quarrel and tells the guys to knock it off.
- Silvia's father, the Duke, enters.
- The Duke chats it up with Proteus and steers the conversation toward Valentine's BFF, Proteus.
- Valentine gushes over his bosom buddy Proteus like a giddy school boy.
- The Duke says it's great that Valentine is so crazy about him because Proteus is on his way here right now.
- Valentine is thrilled and tells Silvia what an awesome guy Proteus is. He also explains that Proteus would have come earlier but he stayed behind for a girl.
- Silvia wonders why Proteus is coming to see *Valentine* if he's so in love with Julia.
- Proteus enters the room and gets a warm welcome from Silvia and Valentine.
- Silvia runs off to speak with her father.
- Valentine confesses that he's in love with Silvia and Proteus takes the opportunity to remind his friend that he *used* to think love was for idiots.
- Proteus and Valentine play a friendly game of "whose girlfriend is the most angelic and saintly creature on earth?" It sounds like this: "My girlfriend is the cutest in all the land." "No, *my* girlfriend is the cutest – yours isn't fit to hold her dress."
- Enough bragging. Valentine confides that he and Silvia are going to run off to Vegas to elope. (OK, they're not going to Vegas, but they are planning to run away and get married.) That night, he'll climb a ladder up to Silvia's window so the couple can run off together. (Hmm. Shakespeare must have really liked this whole "climbing a ladder to a girl's bedroom" thing because he repeats it in *Romeo and Juliet*.)
- Brain Snack: One of Shakespeare's main literary sources for *Two Gentlemen of Verona* is Arthur Brooke's *The Tragicall History of Romeus and Juliet* (1562), which also happens to be the major source for *Romeo and Juliet*.
- Valentine runs off to his room and Proteus says he'll be there in a minute.
- Then Proteus delivers a soliloquy (when a character is alone on stage and delivers a speech that reveals his/her inner thoughts to the audience) about how he has fallen in love with Silvia. (Julia who?) Proteus is a bit torn because he knows his love for a woman will interfere with his bromance with Valentine, who is engaged to Silvia. Finally, Proteus decides he loves Silvia more than Valentine and resolves to win her.

Act 2, Scene 5

- The two servants, Speed and Lance appear on stage with Lance's dog, Crab.
- Speed invites Lance to an alehouse (a bar) and then asks how things went when Proteus said goodbye to Julia. Lance says things went fine. Speed wants to know if they're going to get married.

- As the dialogue continues, Speed can't get a straight answer from Lance, who delivers a series of lines that are loaded with silly puns and dirty jokes.
- Lance announces that if Speed won't go to the alehouse with him, then Speed is a "Jew" and not a Christian.
- (Unfortunately, Lance isn't the only Shakespeare character to utter ugly, anti-Semitic remarks, which are all-too-common in sixteenth-century literature. See, for example, *The Merchant of Venice.*)

Act 2, Scene 6

- Proteus appears alone on stage and delivers a big speech to the audience (a.k.a. a "soliloquy"), which takes up the entire scene. We'll break it down in a second, but the speech boils down to Proteus deciding to do what's best for Proteus.
- At first, Proteus acknowledges that, *if* he leaves Julia and wrongs Proteus by loving "fair Silvia," then he's a jerk. But then, he suggests that "Love" is the culprit here and love is "tempt[ing]" him to betray his girl and his best pal. (Funny how that works out so Proteus is responsible for any of his actions, isn't it?)
- Proteus goes on to say, "At first I did adore a twinkling star,/ But now I worship a celestial sun." Translation: Julia is pretty cute, but Silvia is insanely gorgeous.
- Proteus then rationalizes that the only way he can be true to himself is by betraying Valentine and Julia.
- Proteus then decides that Valentine will be his "enemy" and Julia will be "dead" to him.
- Finally, Proteus resolves to get Valentine in big time trouble with the Duke of Milan – Proteus will tattle to the Duke that Valentine plans to elope with Silvia. The Duke, of course, will be enraged since he's got plans for his daughter to marry Thurio.

Act 2, Scene 7

- Back in Verona, Julia and Lucetta brainstorm about ways for Julia to travel to Milan without losing her "honour." (Remember, girls weren't allowed to go traipsing around the country like the guys do.)
- Lucetta advises Julia to stay home and wait it out – Proteus will be back eventually.
- Julia's not hearing any of this. She's in love and wants to be with Proteus, pronto.
- Julia decides to dress up like a boy to "prevent" any unwanted encounters with "lascivious men" (to protect herself from being raped). She'll tie up her hair in fashionable knots to make her appear older and Lucetta will make her a pair of pants.
- Lucetta advises Julia to also wear a codpiece. (A "codpiece" is a pouch attached to man's breeches that covers the genital area. Codpieces were all the rage in Shakespeare's day.)
- Julia worries that travelling alone and cross-dressing will ruin her reputation, but she

decides that it's worth it because Proteus is the most faithful and loyal guy in the world. (Yeah right.)

- Julia and Lucetta make preparations for the journey.

Act 3, Scene 1

- In Milan, the Duke sends Thurio out of the room so he can have a private conversation with Proteus.
- Proteus then tattles on Valentine for planning to elope with the Duke's daughter. What's worse, Proteus acts like he's betraying Valentine's confidence because the Duke has been such a generous host.
- We learn that the Duke wants Silvia to marry Thurio and that he has suspected all along that his daughter is secretly dating Valentine.
- Proteus asks the Duke not to tell Valentine where he got his information and runs out of the room as Valentine enters.
- Valentine is on his way to Julia's window but the Duke stalls him. The Duke says Julia's a disobedient child and he's thinking of turning her out onto the streets without a dowry.
- That doesn't scare off Valentine so the Duke resorts to lying about being in love with a woman who is engaged to another man. Valentine advises him to elope with her, which basically confirms his own intentions to elope with Silvia.
- The Duke lifts up Valentine's cloak and finds a rope ladder and a love letter to Silvia.
- Furious, he tells Valentine to scram and then storms out of the room.
- Valentine is left alone on stage and delivers his famous "What light is light if Silvia be not seen" soliloquy. (It's all about how life isn't worth living if he can't be with Silvia.)
- Brain Snack: If you've seen the movie *Shakespeare in Love*, you watched Gwyneth Paltrow recite these lines at an audition for Shakespeare's play *Romeo and Juliet*. If you want to see it, go to "Best of the Web" for a links to video clips.
- Proteus and Lance run in and Proteus delivers some bad news: Valentine has been banished. If he's caught in the Duke's court, he'll be put to death.
- Proteus says that Silvia begged her father to relent but the Duke wasn't hearing any of it.
- Proteus, who wants Silvia all for himself, advises Valentine to flee. He offers to deliver Valentine's love letters to Julia, since he's such a great friend and all.
- Valentine is crushed.
- Proteus offers to escort Valentine to the city limits. (What a good friend.)
- Lance enters the stage alone.
- He admits to the audience that he's fallen in love with an unnamed woman and then makes a ridiculous list of her excellent traits: she's better than a hunting dog and a horse because she can do chores around the house. (If you want to know what we think of this, check out "Quotes" for "Marriage.")
- Speed enters and helps Lance with his list of the mystery woman's virtues and vices. Lance and Speed argue about whether or not her "slowness in words" should be listed as

a "vice" or a "virtue." (This is a sexist joke – the so-called ideal woman was supposed to be virtuous, obedient, and *silent*.)
- Speed runs off to meet his master, Valentine.

Act 3, Scene 2

- The Duke of Milan assures Thurio that Silvia will love him now that Valentine is out of the way.
- Thurio whines that Silvia hates him even more now that the love of her life has been banished.
- Proteus enters with news that Valentine is gone.
- The Duke asks Proteus for advice about how to make Silvia forget Valentine.
- Proteus has an idea – he'll talk smack about Valentine whenever Silvia is around. That way, Silvia will be tricked into thinking that Valentine must be a bad guy if his best friend talks trash about him.
- Proteus turns to Thurio and advises him to recite love poetry to Silvia if he wants to win her heart. Thurio should also serenade her outside of her window every night with a band of musicians. (In other words, Proteus is encouraging Thurio to stalk her, which Silvia will hate.)

Act 4, Scene 1

- Meanwhile, Valentine and Speed have fled to a forest between Milan and Mantua, where they encounter a group of outlaws.
- One of the outlaws says "stick em' up" and Valentine proceeds to explain that he's got nothing for the roadside robbers to steal.
- The outlaws are impressed when they hear that Valentine has been banished from Milan. They're even more impressed when Valentine lies about having "killed a man."
- The outlaws now think of Valentine as a kind of Robin Hood figure and invite him to join their bad boy club.
- The outlaws take turns bragging about their crimes.
- Valentine agrees to join the outlaw club but makes them promise not to hurt any women or defenseless travelers. They agree and set off to live as a band of happy bachelors.

Act 4, Scene 2

- Proteus stands outside Silvia's window in the moonlight. He tells the audience Silvia has been spurning his advances. She's also been reminding him of his friendship with Valentine and his commitment to Julia.
- Thurio shows up with a band of musicians and they all serenade Silvia.
- Julia (who is disguised as a young man) enters with the Host, who leads her over to Proteus and the musicians.
- Julia is *not* happy that Proteus is singing to some other girl and she says as much.
- Julia also learns from the Host that Proteus is in love with Silvia.
- Thurio and the musicians take off. Julia watches Proteus try to seduce Silvia.
- Silvia tells Proteus to get lost – he's a disloyal snake.
- Proteus lies and says his girlfriend and Valentine are both dead so there's no reason why they can't be together.
- Silvia promises to give Proteus a picture of her tomorrow if he'll go away and leave her alone.
- Julia is devastated. She's also still wearing her disguise.

Act 4, Scene 3

- The next morning, Silvia asks her dear friend, Eglamour, if he'll travel with her to find Valentine. It's too dangerous for Silvia to travel alone.
- Eglamour knows a thing or two about love and heartbreak so he agrees to help Silvia – they'll meet up tonight at Friar Patrick's cell (room).

Act 4, Scene 4

- Lance and his dog, Crab, are on stage.
- Lance tells the audience a story about how Crab was caught "a pissing" under the Duke's table and Lance took the blame for it so Crab wouldn't be whipped. He also reveals that he once took the blame for Crab when the dog killed a neighbor's geese. Lance begs Crab not pee on any "gentlewoman's" skirt, which seems pretty reasonable.
- Proteus and Julia (disguised as a page boy named "Sebastian") enter.
- Brain Snack: Julia is Shakespeare's first cross-dressing heroine, so we guess we could call her the grandmother of other gender-bending characters that follow in her footsteps – like Viola from *Twelfth Night*, Rosalind from *As You Like It*, and Portia & "Jessica from *The Merchant of Venice.*
- Proteus offers "Sebastian" a job as his errand boy.

- Proteus then questions Speed, who was supposed to have delivered a little lap dog to Julia as a gift.
- It turns out that Speed lost the little dog and tried to offer up Crab instead. Julia refused the gift and sent the dog back.
- Proteus tells Lance to scram and then asks "Sebastian" to deliver a ring to Silvia. (Yep, it's the same ring that Julia gave Proteus before he went away. What a dog.)
- "Sebastian" begins to cry and says Proteus must not have loved the woman who originally gave him the ring. "Sebastian" goes on to say that he feels sorry for the "lady" who gave Proteus the ring – she probably loves Proteus as much as Proteus loves Silvia.
- Proteus is all "whatever – deliver the ring and this letter to Silvia."
- Proteus leaves.
- Poor Julia feels torn – she doesn't see how she can possibly go through with the errand because she's still in love with Proteus. (This is sort of what happens to Viola in *Twelfth Night*. Viola cross-dresses as a boy page and falls in love with her master, Duke Orsino, who asks Viola to deliver love letters to another woman.)
- Silvia enters and begins to chat with "Sebastian."
- "Sebastian" hands over a love letter and then immediately asks for it back, explaining that "he" gave Silvia the wrong letter. (We're not sure what the first letter said, but it's probably a letter that Proteus wrote to *Julia*. Did Julia/Sebastian do this on purpose?)
- "Sebastian" gives Silvia the letter intended for her and Silvia promptly tears it up. She also refuses to take the ring because she knows that it was given to Proteus by Julia.
- Silvia feels pity for Julia and asks "Sebastian" if he knows her. "Sebastian" says that, yes, "he" knows Julia – she used to be very pretty but now that Proteus has dumped her, she's not looking or feeling so hot.
- Silvia wants to know more about Julia, so "Sebastian" says "he" and Julia are the same height. In fact, "he" once wore her clothes when "he" played the role of a woman, Ariadne, in a church play. "Sebastian's" performance of this "woman's part" was so good that it moved Julia to tears.
- Brain Snack: Ariadne is a figure from Greek mythology. She's famous for hanging herself after her boyfriend, Theseus, dumped her. Now, we know that Julia/Sebastian never played the role of Ariadne in a play. This made up story is Julia's only way of expressing her sadness over the loss of Proteus.
- Silvia is so moved by "Sebastian's" story that she gives the pageboy a bag full of money before she leaves. (Aww. How sweet.)
- Julia is left alone on stage to gaze at the picture Silvia has left behind for Proteus. Poor Julia admires Silvia's beauty and wonders if Proteus would love her more if she looked more like Silvia.
- Then Julia says that it's a good thing Silvia turned out to be so nice – otherwise, she would have "scratched out" her eyes.

Act 5, Scene 1

- At Friar Patrick's cell, Eglamour patiently waits for Silvia, who has planned to meet him there.
- Silvia rushes in and says they need to hurry because she's afraid spies have been following her.
- They run off to the forest between Milan and Mantua. (Yep, that's the same forest where Valentine is hanging out with his new outlaw pals.)

Act 5, Scene 2

- At the Duke's court in Milan, Thurio asks Proteus to tell him what Silvia thinks of him. Proteus says that Silvia doesn't like it when Thurio opens his mouth to speak but, other than that, she seems to be warming up to him.
- "Sebastian" stands next to Proteus muttering insults that only the audience can hear. (This technique is called an "aside," by the way.)
- The Duke storms in and announces that Eglamour and Silvia have run off to find that loser Valentine. Everyone should grab their gear and horses so they can help track down the runaways.
- Thurio says he'll go along but only to punish Eglamour – he's not really into Silvia anymore.

Act 5, Scene 3

- In the forest, the three outlaws have captured Silvia and plan to take her to their leader (that would be Valentine).
- The Third Outlaw says something like, "Don't worry, our leader isn't going to assault you."
- We also learn that when Eglamour saw the outlaws, he hightailed it out of there, leaving Silvia to fend for herself.
- Silvia rolls her eyes and says she's enduring all of this for Valentine.

Act 5, Scene 4

- In another part of the forest, Valentine is alone and contemplates the perks of forest living. He likes the solitude and the sounds of nature because he can think about his love for Silvia without being disturbed. Plus, he doesn't have to deal with the chaos of court life.

- The only downside to this new lifestyle is that baby sitting his new outlaw buddies is hard work – he's always busy preventing them from robbing and assaulting hapless travelers.
- Proteus, Silvia, and Julia (dressed as "Sebastian") enter the stage. Valentine sees them but they don't see him.
- Proteus, who has apparently rescued Silvia from the outlaws, insists that Silvia should be grateful – if he hadn't come along, they would have ravaged her.
- Silvia says she would have rather been eaten by a lion than rescued by the "false Proteus."
- Silvia tells Proteus to go back to Julia. He should also be a better friend to Valentine.
- Proteus replies that if Silvia won't love him, he'll "woo [her] like a soldier, at arms end,/ And love [her] 'gainst the nature of love: force [her]." Translation: he's going to rape her.
- Before Proteus can assault Silvia, Valentine rushes over and stops him.
- Instead of yelling at Proteus for trying to rape Silvia, Valentine lights him up for being a lousy friend. (We're not kidding. Valentine is more concerned about Proteus's betrayal of friendship than he is about the fact that his pal is a would-be rapist.)
- Proteus apologizes for being a disloyal friend to Valentine and Valentine forgives him immediately.
- To demonstrate his affection for Proteus, Valentine says "All that was mine in Silvia I give thee." There are a couple of ways to read this: 1) Any claims I made to Silvia's love, I give thee. (He's going to step aside and let Proteus have her.) or 2) All the love I gave to Silvia, I'll give to you too. (He'll love Proteus and Silvia equally.)
- Brain Snack: In the story of Titus and Gisippus (related first by Boccaccio and later retold in Thomas Elyot's *Book of the Governor* (1531), Gisippus gives his best friend, Titus, the woman he is supposed to marry after Titus falls in love with her (*Book Named the Governor*, 2.12). This story, as you can guess, was a major literary influence on Shakespeare's play.
- Before Proteus can respond, "Sebastian" faints.
- "Sebastian" then snaps out of it and reveals that "he" is actually Julia. Plus, Julia has got the ring Proteus gave her to prove it.
- Now that "Sebastian" is Julia again, Julia says "Ha! You're busted."
- Proteus feels guilty for having strayed from Julia and says he doesn't know what he was thinking – now that he sees Julia again, he's back in love with her.
- This, apparently, is enough for Julia to forgive Proteus. They join hands.
- The outlaws burst onto the scene with a couple of prisoners – the Duke and Thurio.
- Thurio tries to grab Silvia and Valentine threatens to kill him. (Gosh. Where were the death threats when Proteus had Silvia?)
- Thurio is like, "Fine, you can have her because I don't want her."
- The Duke is so impressed by Valentine that he lifts Valentine's banishment and announces that he can have his daughter – it'll be his "gift" to Valentine.
- Valentine thanks the Duke for the generous "gift" and announces that the outlaws should be pardoned for all their past crimes.
- Fine, says the Duke.
- Now that that's settled, everyone sets off for the Duke's court in Milan. Valentine gets all buddy-buddy with his father-in-law to be by promising to tell the Duke a funny story about

how Julia wound up dressed like a boy in the middle of the forest.

- Valentine proposes to have a double wedding and everyone heads back to Milan for a big shindig.
- Check out "What's Up With the Ending?" if you want to know more…

Themes

Theme of Friendship

Two Gentlemen of Verona is often described as a "celebration" of male friendship. In the play, male bonds are threatened by heterosexual romance and one man's capacity for betrayal. While some critics read the play as an attempt to reconcile the tension between friendship and heterosexual love, others see a play in which male bonds are given priority over all other relationships. We can also read the play as an exploration of common sixteenth-century attitudes. For many prominent writers and philosophers, male friendship was considered the most elevated form of human connectedness. Shakespeare's portrayal of male bonds in *Two Gentlemen* echoes throughout his other works – especially the *Sonnets*, *The Merchant of Venice*, and *The Winter's Tale* .

Questions About Friendship

1. Why is Proteus so sad to see his friend leave Verona?
2. What is it, exactly, that threatens to break up Proteus and Valentine's relationship?
3. Describe Valentine's response to Proteus's attempt to rape Silvia.
4. Why do you think Valentine offers to "give" Silvia to Proteus?

Chew on Friendship

In the play, the bonds of male friendship are threatened by the male characters' romantic interests in women.

Even after Valentine is formally engaged to Silvia, his loyalty to Proteus remains his first priority.

Theme of Love

Love makes men and women do some pretty strange things in *Two Gentlemen of Verona*. It turns men and women into fickle creatures and has the potential to transform men into unrecognizable and lovesick fools, or worse. At the same time, in Valentine and Silvia, we see two young lovers willing to risk everything to be together – an idea that Shakespeare will later develop in *Romeo and Juliet* . Romantic love between men and women, of course, is also pitted

against the bonds of male friendship.

Questions About Love

1. Why does Proteus stay behind in Verona instead of traveling the "world" with Valentine?
2. Why does Silvia ask Valentine to write a love letter to her "friend"?
3. How does romantic love get in the way of friendship in the play?
4. Why does Proteus fall back in love with Julia and why does he take her back?

Chew on Love

In the play, love turns men and women into fickle creatures.

Lance's devotion to his ungrateful dog Crab is a parody of the romantic relationships in the play.

Although the play ends with the promise of a double wedding, romantic love in *Two Gentlemen of Verona* plays second fiddle to male friendship.

Theme of Transformation

Like a lot of Shakespeare plays, *The Two Gentlemen of Verona* toys with the common sixteenth-century notion that love can transform men and women (but mostly men) into something unrecognizable. Ultimately, however, such transformations *reveal* more about characters' identities than the transformations conceal. The clearest example of this is when the disclosure of Julia's "Sebastian" disguise prompts Proteus to discover something about himself as he declares "O heaven! were man/ But constant, he were perfect" (5.4.7). The point seems to be that, while human beings can be fickle, changeable, and unstable, they are also capable of some pretty important self-revelations.

Questions About Transformation

1. Which characters undergo some kind of transformation in the play? (What *kinds* of metamorphoses do characters experience?)
2. Why does Julia transform herself by donning a disguise?
3. How does Proteus's fickle nature relate to the theme of transformation?
4. If love transforms the men and women who fall under its spell, does it change them for the better?

Chew on Transformation

Romantic love has the capacity to transform men and women into monsters.

Julia's transformation from "Sebastian" back into "Julia" is the catalyst for Proteus's realization that his changeable nature is his worst a flaw.

Theme of Violence

Two Gentlemen of Verona culminates in an attempted rape that is narrowly averted and quickly forgiven. In fact, the threat of sexual violence seems to echo all throughout the play. Proteus's attempt to rape Silvia is preceded by a reference to the mythical Philomela's rape by Tereus (5.4.1), Valentine makes the outlaws swear to "do no outrages/ On silly women" (4.1.12), and Julia disguises herself as "Sebastian" so she can avoid "loose encounters of lascivious men" (2.7.4). In the play, the threat of rape seems to be symptomatic of a world in which men see women as objects to be possessed, stolen, or bestowed upon other men as "gifts."

Questions About Violence

1. What is Julia hoping to avoid by dressing up as a boy before she travels to Milan?
2. Why does Valentine forgive Proteus so easily after he attempts to rape Silvia?
3. Are there any consequences for Proteus's attempted sexual assault?
4. Is the forest a safe place for women?

Chew on Violence

In the play, Proteus's attempt to sexually assault Silvia is symptomatic of a world in which men view women as possessions to be traded, gifted, or stolen.

Proteus's attempt to rape Silvia threatens to turn Shakespeare's comedy into a tragedy.

Theme of Lies and Deceit

Deception, disguise, and betrayal are par for the course in *Two Gentlemen of Verona*. When characters disguise their identities and/or their true intentions, the result is a plot with the kinds of twists and turns that we've come to expect from Shakespeare's comedies. The play is also interested in the moral and philosophical aspects of deception (although, it handles the theme with a pretty light hand). While some lovers play silly mind games, Proteus betrays his best friend and girlfriend by going after Silvia. In the play, it seems that the betrayal of male friendship is one of the worst crimes imaginable. (Strangely enough, the play also suggests that it's even worse than attempted rape.)

Questions About Lies and Deceit

1. Why don't Silvia and Valentine come clean about their relationship to Silvia's father, the Duke of Milan? What are the consequences of their secrecy?
2. How does Proteus deceive Valentine?
3. Why does Julia remain in her "Sebastian" disguise for so long? Why not reveal her identity as soon as she finds Proteus?
4. Does Julia's deception ever allow any truths to come to light?

Chew on Lies and Deceit

Although Julia's "Sebastian" disguise deceives those around her, the disguise also allows her to speak the truth about her feelings for Proteus.

By the play's end, Proteus believes that his betrayal of Valentine is the worst kind of deception there is – it's even worse than his betrayal of Julia.

Theme of Gender

In *Two Gentlemen of Verona*, we see some blatantly sexist attitudes that echo common sixteenth-century attitudes toward women. In the play, various characters suggest that women are fickle, deceptive, incapable of meaningful relationships, and have the capacity to transform the men into fools. Women are also treated as personal property in the play. However, at the same time that women are treated as property that can be stolen, traded, or bestowed to other men as "gifts," the play *also* seems to hint at the dangers of viewing women this way. Shakespeare also creates two very strong heroines in Julia and Silvia, who are gutsy, loyal, and steadfast. In the play, Shakespeare also draws our attention to the slipperiness of gender when Julia cross-dresses and passes herself off as "Sebastian."

Questions About Gender

1. What preparations must Julia make before she travels? Do the male characters ever take similar precautions?
2. How does "Sebastian" blur traditional ideas about gender?
3. How would you describe the play's overall attitude toward women? Do you think the play's female characters are more admirable than the male characters?
4. Why does Thurio say he no longer wishes to marry Silvia in Act 5, Scene 4?

Chew on Gender

In the play, Proteus, Valentine, and the Duke see women as objects that can be possessed, stolen, or exchanged as "gifts" between men.

In the play, Silvia and Julia are the most admirable characters because they're gutsy and loyal.

Theme of Marriage

Marriage between a man and a woman is the union that all of Shakespeare's comedies work toward. In order to achieve such a union, the characters in *Two Gentlemen of Verona* must overcome several obstacles – disagreeable parents, the fickleness of romance, love triangles, deception, and betrayal. Looked at from another angle, however, the pursuit of marriage in the play is the major obstacle standing in the way of male friendship. Although the play ends in the promise of a double wedding, it's not clear whether or not marriage between a man and a woman ever trumps male friendship as the most important human bond.

Questions About Marriage

1. Why do Valentine and Silvia want to elope? What's standing in their way?
2. What is the function of Lance's announcement that he's fallen in love with a woman with "more qualities than a water-spaniel"? What does this suggest about the character's attitude toward marriage? Does it shed any light on how the main characters (like Proteus and Valentine) feel about love and marriage?
3. How is Silvia's engagement to Valentine arranged?
4. Read the final lines of the play and discuss the implications of Valentine's statement: "our day of marriage shall be yours;/ One feast, one house, one mutual happiness" (5.4.14).

Chew on Marriage

Although *Two Gentlemen* promises a double wedding at the end of Act 5, Scene 4, the play also leaves us wondering if Proteus and Valentine will value their marriages as much as they honor their friendship with each other.

Although Julia is ashamed about cross-dressing, her social impropriety is excusable because Julia's actions are in the interest of her getting married.

Theme of Society and Class

While some earlier sixteenth-century plays portray servants as shadows of the main characters (minor characters and servants often mimicked their masters' behaviors), Shakespeare does something relatively new in *Two Gentlemen of Verona*. In the play, the servants' attitudes towards marriage, love, loyalty, and social standing often call attention to the foibles of their masters. Shakespeare, then, is probably the first playwright to portray servants who are capable

of defining the main characters. For example, Lance's devotion to his dog Crab draws our attention to Proteus's disloyalty to Julia and Valentine. The servants in *Two Gentlemen* are more than mere sounding boards and offer much more than mere comic relief.

Questions About Society and Class

1. How would you characterize Julia's relationship with Lucetta? What about Valentine's relationship to his servant, Speed? Proteus's relationship with Lance?
2. How does Antonio respond to Panthino's advice to send Proteus abroad?
3. Why does Shakespeare go out of his way to dramatize Lance's devotion to his dog, Crab? What's the effect when Lance asks questions like "How many masters would do this for his servant" (4.4.1)?
4. What's the difference between Lance's love for the unnamed woman he falls for in Act 3, Scene 1 and Valentine's love for Silvia?

Chew on Society and Class

In *Two Gentlemen of Verona,* the servants offer much more than comic relief – they function as foils to their masters.

The actions and speeches of Lance, Speed, and Lucetta reveal the foolishness and folly of the main characters.

Friendship Quotes

Wilt thou be gone? Sweet Valentine, adieu!
Think on thy Proteus, when thou haply seest
Some rare note-worthy object in thy travel:
Wish me partaker in thy happiness
When thou dost meet good hap; and in thy danger,
If ever danger do environ thee,
Commend thy grievance to my holy prayers,
For I will be thy beadsman, Valentine. (1.1.1)

Thought: It's pretty clear from the play's beginning that Valentine and Proteus are devoted friends. As the two bosom buddies say goodbye, Proteus promises to pray for Valentine and says he hopes Valentine will think of him during his travels.

In Shakespeare's day, male friendship was considered one of the most sacred and important

bonds. In a famous book published in 1531, Thomas Elyot writes that "he semeth to take the sun from the world, that taketh friendship from man's life" (*The Book Named the Governor*, 2.11).

I know him as myself; for from our infancy
We have conversed and spent our hours together: (2.4.20)

Thought: Here, Valentine explains why he and Proteus are so close – the pair have known each other since infancy and have spent their entire lives together. When Proteus says "I know him as myself," he means to suggest that he knows Proteus *as well as* he knows himself. At the same time, the phrase, "I know him *as myself*" seems to also suggest that Proteus and Valentine are like two halves of the same being. Valentine seems to be echoing a common sixteenth-century idea made famous by Thomas Elyot's *The Book Named the Governor*. In Book 2, Chapter 11, Elyot says that friendship makes "two persons one in having and suffering. And therefore a friend is properly named of philosophers the other I. For that in them is but one mind and one possession" (2.11).

This passage from *Two Gentlemen of Verona* also reminds us of the childhood friendship between Leontes and Polixenes's in Shakespeare's later play, *The Winter's Tale.* When Polixenes describes his friendship with Leontes, he says they were like "twinn'd lambs that did frisk i' the sun" (*Winter's Tale,* 1.2.10), which is a very sweet way to describe the "innocence" and joy of a carefree childhood friendship between two boys. It also implies that Polixenes and Leontes were so close that they were practically *identical* ("twinn'd").

Even as one heat another heat expels,
Or as one nail by strength drives out another,
So the remembrance of my former love
Is by a newer object quite forgotten.
[...]
She is fair; and so is Julia that I love--
That I did love, for now my love is thaw'd;
[...]
Methinks my zeal to Valentine is cold,
And that I love him not as I was wont.
O, but I love his lady too too much,
And that's the reason I love him so little. (2.4.18)

Thought: Uh-oh. This is where Proteus tells the audience he's fallen in love with his best friend's girlfriend, which means he's fallen *out* of love with Julia. He's also lost his "zeal" for Valentine. Notice the way Proteus talks about falling in and out of love as losing "heat" (passion, love, desire, etc.) and going cold? Proteus says his love for Julia has "thawed" and his "zeal to

Valentine is *cold*" (our emphasis). Question: why do you think Proteus uses the same terminology to describe falling out of love with his girlfriend and loving his best friend "so little"?

DUKE
What might we do to make the girl forget
The love of Valentine and love Sir Thurio?
PROTEUS
The best way is to slander Valentine
With falsehood, cowardice and poor descent,
Three things that women highly hold in hate. (3.2.7)

Thought: Once Proteus loses his "zeal" for Valentine (see above passage), he quickly stabs his friend in the back. At this point, he has not only gotten Valentine kicked out of court (by telling the Duke Valentine planned to elope with Silvia), he's also resorted to "slander" in the hopes that trash talking Valentine to Silvia will help him win her heart.

SILVIA
The more shame for him that he sends it me;
For I have heard him say a thousand times
His Julia gave it him at his departure.
Though his false finger have profaned the ring,
Mine shall not do his Julia so much wrong.
JULIA
She thanks you. (4.4.4)

Thought: As one critic puts it, Shakespeare is definitely interested in "celebrating" male friendship in this play. But, when we read this passage from *Two Gentlemen of Verona,* we can't help but think that Shakespeare hints that women are capable of friendship too. Here, Silvia refuses to accept the ring Proteus has sent her (by way of Julia, who is disguised as a page boy, "Sebastian"). Silvia insists that she would never do "Julia so much wrong," which gestures at Silvia's capacity for loyalty and solidarity with another woman. (Unlike Proteus, who is busy stabbing his best friend in the back.)

I dare not say
I have one friend alive; thou wouldst disprove me.
Who should be trusted, when one's own right hand
Is perjured to the bosom? Proteus,
I am sorry I must never trust thee more,
But count the world a stranger for thy sake.
The private wound is deepest: O time most accurst,

'Mongst all foes that a friend should be the worst! (5.4.4)

Thought: Immediately after Valentine prevents Proteus from raping Silvia, Valentine lays into his friend. The surprising thing is that Valentine doesn't yell at Proteus for being a potential rapist. He yells at him for being such a disloyal friend. Valentine is more upset about not being able to "trust" his pal than he is outraged that Proteus would assault a woman. What's up with that?

My shame and guilt confounds me.
Forgive me, Valentine: if hearty sorrow
Be a sufficient ransom for offence,
I tender 't here; I do as truly suffer
As e'er I did commit. (5.4.4)

Thought: After being caught red-handed trying to rape Silvia, Proteus immediately apologizes…to*Valentine*. Proteus never expresses remorse for his crime against Silvia. He feels bad because he hurt Valentine's feelings and betrayed his friend's trust. If you think that's bad, keep reading, because it gets even worse.

Then I am paid;
And once again I do receive thee honest.
Who by repentance is not satisfied
Is nor of heaven nor earth, for these are pleased.
By penitence the Eternal's wrath's appeased:
and, that my love may appear plain and free,
All that was mine in Silvia I give thee. (5.4.5)

Thought: Valentine forgives Proteus for trying to rape Silvia pretty quickly. What's interesting about this passage is the way Valentine seems to offer to "give" Silvia to his friend as a peace offering and a gesture of friendship. Despite Proteus's behavior and despite Valentine's love for Silvia, Valentine prioritizes his friendship with Proteus over all else – especially his girlfriend.

This is similar to what happens in one of Shakespeare's main literary source for his play. In the story of Titus and Gisippus – related first by Boccaccio and later retold in Thomas Elyot's *Book of the Governor* (1531) – Gisippus gives his best friend, Titus, the woman he is supposed to marry after Titus falls in love with her (*Book Named the Governor*, 2.12).

DUKE
Thou art a gentleman and well derived;
Take thou thy Silvia, for thou hast deserved her.
VALENTINE

I thank your grace; the gift hath made me happy.
I now beseech you, for your daughter's sake,
To grant one boom that I shall ask of you.
[...]
These banish'd men that I have kept withal
Are men endued with worthy qualities:
Forgive them what they have committed here
And let them be recall'd from their exile: (5.4.1)

Thought: Gosh. Valentine and the Duke sure are buddy-buddy in this passage. We also notice that when the Duke offers to let Valentine marry his daughter, Valentine seems more interested in helping out his new outlaw friends than in celebrating his engagement to Silvia.

Come, Proteus; 'tis your penance but to hear
The story of your loves discovered:
That done, our day of marriage shall be yours;
One feast, one house, one mutual happiness. (5.4.14)

Thought: In the end, Proteus falls back in love with Julia (who takes him back) and Valentine and Silvia are engaged with the Duke's blessing. (This is typical of Shakespearean comedy. At the end of his comedies, Shakespeare always marries someone off, which you can read more about by going to "Genre.") Here, Valentine tells Proteus they should all celebrate by having a *double* wedding. Does this mean that Valentine's bromance with Proteus is being replaced by his marriage to Silvia? Not necessarily. Valentine says the double wedding will be "one feast, one house, one mutual happiness." "One mutual happiness"? Is Valentine talking about the mutual happiness between husband and wife? Or is he talking about the mutual happiness between him and Proteus?

Love Quotes

Were't not affection chains thy tender days
To the sweet glances of thy honour'd love,
I rather would entreat thy company
To see the wonders of the world abroad, (1.1.1)

Thought: Valentine wishes that his best friend would join him to "see the wonders of the world abroad," but Proteus's love for Julia prevents his friend from leaving Verona.

To be in love, where scorn is bought with groans;
Coy looks with heart-sore sighs; one fading moment's mirth
With twenty watchful, weary, tedious nights:
If haply won, perhaps a hapless gain;
If lost, why then a grievous labour won;
However, but a folly bought with wit,
Or else a wit by folly vanquished. (1.1.6)

Thought: At the beginning of the play, Valentine is cynical about love. If a man succeeds in winning a woman's heart, he says, it is a "hapless gain." On the other hand, if a man loses in love, it's a "labour won."

I leave myself, my friends and all, for love.
Thou, Julia, thou hast metamorphosed me,
Made me neglect my studies, lose my time,
War with good counsel, set the world at nought;
Made wit with musing weak, heart sick with thought. (1.1.11)

Thought: Proteus declares that his love for Julia has transformed him. Ever since he fell in love with Julia, Proteus doesn't study, he argues with his friends, and isn't very witty. Understood this way, love does not change one for the better.

This passage seems to anticipate what famous essayist Francis Bacon later writes (c. 1600) about male-female love: "You may observe, that amongst all the great and worthy persons (whereof the memory remaineth, either ancient or recent) there is not one, that hath been transported to the mad degree of love: which shows that great spirits, and great business, do keep out this weak passion" (Francis Bacon, "Of Love").

JULIA
His little speaking shows his love but small.
LUCETTA
Fire that's closest kept burns most of all.
JULIA
They do not love that do not show their love.
LUCETTA
O, they love least that let men know their love. (1.2.11)

Thought: Julia thinks that a man's love can be measured by the words he speaks, as if love is somehow quantifiable. This sort of reminds us of King Lear, who famously asks his daughters, "Which of you shall we say doth love us most?" (*King Lear*, 1.1.2).

Sweet love! sweet lines! sweet life!
Here is her hand, the agent of her heart;
Here is her oath for love, her honour's pawn.
O, that our fathers would applaud our loves,
To seal our happiness with their consents!
O heavenly Julia! (1.3.6)

Thought: Proteus is madly in love with Julia and wishes that their dads would get on board with their relationship. In the play (and in Shakespeare's time), young couples typically married only after their fathers' gave permission.

Marry, by these special marks: first, you have
learned, like Sir Proteus, to wreathe your arms,
like a malecontent; to relish a love-song, like a
robin-redbreast; to walk alone, like one that had
the pestilence; to sigh, like a school-boy that had
lost his A B C; to weep, like a young wench that had
buried her grandam; to fast, like one that takes
diet; to watch like one that fears robbing; to
speak puling, like a beggar at Hallowmas. You were
wont, when you laughed, to crow like a cock; when you
walked, to walk like one of the lions; when you
fasted, it was presently after dinner; when you
looked sadly, it was for want of money: and now you
are metamorphosed with a mistress, that, when I look
on you, I can hardly think you my master. (2.1.8)

Thought: When Valentine travels to Milan, he falls in love with Silvia. (So much for the cynical Valentine we saw in Act 1, Scene 1.) Here, Speed mocks him for having been "metamorphosed" by love and suggests that Valentine has changed so much that he's hardly recognizable.

Nay, then he should be blind; and, being blind
How could he see his way to seek out you? (2.4.23)

Thought: Silvia raises an excellent question. If Proteus loves Julia so much, why is he leaving her in Verona and travelling to Milan, where his best friend Valentine is hanging out? The easy answer is that Proteus's dad is making him. Still, Silvia's shrewd question seems to gesture at the fact that Proteus isn't as dedicated to Julia as he claims to be.

Methinks my zeal to Valentine is cold,
And that I love him not as I was wont.
O, but I love his lady too too much,
And that's the reason I love him so little.
How shall I dote on her with more advice,
That thus without advice begin to love her! (2.4.18)

Thought: For Proteus, falling out of love with Julia means that his "zeal" to Valentine is "cold." In the play, it seems like a man's romantic interests always threaten to break up his friendships with other men. It's also pretty clear that Proteus is fickle – he easily falls in and out of love.

Then let me go and hinder not my course
I'll be as patient as a gentle stream
And make a pastime of each weary step,
Till the last step have brought me to my love;
And there I'll rest, as after much turmoil
A blessed soul doth in Elysium. (2.7.3)

Thought: Although Proteus falls out of love with Julia as easy as we might change a pair of socks, Julia's devotion to Proteus is pretty rock steady – she willing to risk everything to follow Proteus to Milan so the couple can be together. Here, she declares that her reunion with Proteus will be just like heaven.

And why not death rather than living torment?
To die is to be banish'd from myself;
And Silvia is myself: banish'd from her
Is self from self: a deadly banishment!
What light is light, if Silvia be not seen?
What joy is joy, if Silvia be not by?
Unless it be to think that she is by
And feed upon the shadow of perfection
Except I be by Silvia in the night,
There is no music in the nightingale;
Unless I look on Silvia in the day,
There is no day for me to look upon;
She is my essence, and I leave to be,
If I be not by her fair influence
Foster'd, illumined, cherish'd, kept alive.
I fly not death, to fly his deadly doom:
Tarry I here, I but attend on death:
but, fly I hence, I fly away from life. (3.1.15)

Thought: This is one of the most famous speeches in the play. Here, Valentine laments that he's been banished from Milan and his beloved Silvia. In elevated terms, he declares that life is meaningless for him without her, so much so that fleeing from Milan is the same as "fly[ing] away from life." This reminds of the character "Juliet," who says that Romeo's banishment is like a death sentence (*Romeo and Juliet*, 3.2.10).

All that was mine in Silvia I give thee. (5.4.5)

Thought: After Proteus apologizes to Valentine for trying to steal his girlfriend, Valentine immediately forgives him and makes a peace offering. There seems to be a few ways to read this passage:

1. Any claims I made to Silvia's love, I give thee. (He's going to step aside and let Proteus have her.
2. All the love I gave to Silvia, I give thee. (Valentine loves Proteus more than he loves Silvia.)
3. All the love I gave to Silvia, I'll give to you too. (He'll love Proteus and Silvia equally.)

Either way, things aren't looking too good for Silvia, who was nearly raped by Proteus and is about to get formally engaged to a guy who doesn't place her first.

Transformation Quotes
I leave myself, my friends and all, for love.
Thou, Julia, thou hast metamorphosed me,
Made me neglect my studies, lose my time,
War with good counsel, set the world at nought;
Made wit with musing weak, heart sick with thought. (1.1.11)

Thought: Proteus claims that his love for Julia has transformed him, and not in a good way. Ever since Julia came along, he no longer does his homework, he wastes all of his time, and he argues with his friends. What's more, Proteus claims that love has also made him weak witted (stupid).

Marry, by these special marks: first, you have
learned, like Sir Proteus, to wreathe your arms,
like a malecontent; to relish a love-song, like a
robin-redbreast; to walk alone, like one that had
the pestilence; to sigh, like a school-boy that had
lost his A B C; to weep, like a young wench that had
buried her grandam; to fast, like one that takes
diet; to watch like one that fears robbing; to
speak puling, like a beggar at Hallowmas. You were

wont, when you laughed, to crow like a cock; when you
walked, to walk like one of the lions; when you
fasted, it was presently after dinner; when you
looked sadly, it was for want of money: and now you
are metamorphosed with a mistress, that, when I look
on you, I can hardly think you my master. (2.1.8)

Thought: When Valentine falls for Silvia, Speed accuses him of being so "metamorphosed" by love that he can hardly recognize Valentine as his master. Speed's laundry list of comparisons (Valentine *used* to walk like a "lion" but now he weeps like a "young wench," and so on) emphasizes Speed's point – Valentine has undergone a complete transformation. We see this same idea in plays like *A Midsummer Night's Dream* and *Taming of the Shrew*, where love has the capacity to alter those who are under its spell.

SPEED
You never saw her since she was deformed.
VALENTINE
How long hath she been deformed?
SPEED
Ever since you loved her.
VALENTINE
I have loved her ever since I saw her; and still I
see her beautiful.
SPEED
If you love her, you cannot see her. (2.1.18)

Thought: Valentine thinks Silvia is the most beautiful woman on earth, but, here, Speed deflates his love for Silvia by insisting that love has "blinded" Valentine, or has at least impaired his vision. Speed insists that, by falling in love with Julia, Valentine caused Julia to be "deformed." Translation: Valentine is wearing love goggles, which distorts Valentine's image of her.

SILVIA
What, angry, Sir Thurio! do you change colour?
VALENTINE
Give him leave, madam; he is a kind of chameleon.
THURIO
That hath more mind to feed on your blood than live
in your air. (2.4.3)

Thought: Thurio is so enraged by Valentine and Silvia's flirtatious relationship that his face turns red. Silvia, being the sassy girl that she is, makes fun of him and Valentine piles on the insults by calling Thurio a "chameleon," a creature with the capacity to change color. Is Valentine also suggesting that Thurio has a fickle personality? If so, he might be right because, later in the play, Thurio decides he's no longer interested in a "peevish" girl (5.2.33).

LUCETTA
But in what habit will you go along?
JULIA
Not like a woman; for I would prevent
The loose encounters of lascivious men:
Gentle Lucetta, fit me with such weeds
As may beseem some well-reputed page. (2.7.4)

Thought: Julia is determined to follow Proteus to Milan, but, as a woman, travelling alone is a big no-no. The solution? To transform her appearance by disguising herself as a boy.

She hath been fairer, madam, than she is:
When she did think my master loved her well,
She, in my judgment, was as fair as you:
But since she did neglect her looking-glass
And threw her sun-expelling mask away,
The air hath starved the roses in her cheeks
And pinch'd the lily-tincture of her face,
That now she is become as black as I. (4.4.17)

Thought: Disguised as "Sebastian," Julia reveals to Silvia that she feels her love for Proteus has physically transformed her. At one time, she was a beauty but, since Proteus betrayed her, Julia says she has neglected her appearances. Julia's remarks are a bit ironic, given that she's wearing a disguise that literally *has* changed her looks. At the same time, Julia's sense that she has become physically unattractive is probably a reflection of how heartache makes her feel on the inside.

We also want to point out that Julia's comments about no longer being fair (light-complexioned and good-looking) because she hasn't protected her skin from the sun's rays reflects a common sixteenth-century idea in England – that light skin is more attractive than dark skin. One of the clearest examples of this attitude can be seen in the words of several characters in *Othello*.

How use doth breed a habit in a man!
This shadowy desert, unfrequented woods,
I better brook than flourishing peopled towns:
Here can I sit alone, unseen of any,
And to the nightingale's complaining notes
Tune my distresses and record my woes. (5.4.1)

Thought: When Valentine gets kicked out of Milan for trying to elope with the Duke's daughter, he bums around a forest, where he finds a sense of peace bemoaning his sadness in harmony with the mournful sounds of the nightingale. As literary scholar Jean Howard reminds us, Valentine's reference to the nightingale recalls the mythic story of Philomela, who was raped by Tereus and eventually transformed into a nightingale whose sad tune mourned the loss of Philomela's virginity. OK, we know what you're thinking. What does the mythic story of Philomela's rape and transformation into a bird have to do with Valentine hanging out in the forest missing his girlfriend? Well, it can't be a coincidence that moments after Valentine mentions the nightingale, his pal Proteus tries to rape Silvia in the very same forest, can it? Keep reading…

Nay, if the gentle spirit of moving words
Can no way change you to a milder form,
I'll woo you like a soldier, at arms' end,
And love you 'gainst the nature of love,--force ye. (5.4.5)

Thought: Here, Proteus says that, if he can't transform Julia's feelings for him, then he'll resort to rape. It seems like Proteus has been transformed himself – into an animal. See "Quotes" for "Violence" if you want to know more about the attempted rape.

O Proteus, let this habit make thee blush!
Be thou ashamed that I have took upon me
Such an immodest raiment, if shame live
In a disguise of love:
It is the lesser blot, modesty finds,
Women to change their shapes than men their minds. (5.4.7)

Thought: Julia is pretty embarrassed that she had to resort to "chang[ing]" her "shape" (dressing as a boy) in order to chase down Proteus. But here, she tells Proteus that he should be even more "ashamed" by his infidelity ("chang[ing]" his "mind" about her and pursuing Silvia). Keep reading for Proteus's response to this…

PROTEUS
Than men their minds! 'tis true.
O heaven! were man
But constant, he were perfect. (5.4.7)

Thought: After Julia reveals her true identity as a woman and declares that it's worse for men to change "their minds" than for women to "change their shapes" (cross-dress), Proteus suddenly realizes that Julia is right about his behavior – he's been falling in and out of love and his inconstancy makes him flawed. Literary scholar Marjorie Garber points out that, at this moment in the play, Proteus's true nature is "unmasked" at the exact same time that Julia's true identity has been revealed (*Shakespeare After All*, 46).

Violence Quotes

LUCETTA
But in what habit will you go along?
JULIA
Not like a woman; for I would prevent
The loose encounters of lascivious men:
Gentle Lucetta, fit me with such weeds
As may beseem some well-reputed page. (2.7.5)

Thought: Julia dons a disguise while she travels to Milan in order to ward off "lascivious" men who might attack a woman travelling alone.

Know, then, that some of us are gentlemen,
Such as the fury of ungovern'd youth
Thrust from the company of awful men:
Myself was from Verona banished
For practising to steal away a lady,
An heir, and near allied unto the duke. (4.1.6)

Thought: The Third Outlaw reveals something peculiar when he explains to Valentine why he was banished from the court – he got kicked out for trying to "steal away a lady." There are a couple of ways to read this. On the one hand, we can assume that the outlaw was planning on eloping with a woman (like Valentine was planning to elope with Silvia). On the other hand, we could read the phrase "to steal away a lady" as a confession of an attempted assault.

I take your offer and will live with you,
Provided that you do no outrages
On silly women or poor passengers. (4.1.12)

Thought: Valentine agrees to be the outlaws' leader, on the condition that that they "do no outrages" on women. What kind of "outrages" is he afraid they'll commit, exactly? Robbery? Rape? Something else? No wonder Julia was so afraid to travel alone.

But when I look on her perfections,
There is no reason but I shall be blind.
If I can cheque my erring love, I will;
If not, to compass her I'll use my skill. (2.4.18)

Thought: This is one of the first hints of Proteus's capacity for sexual violence. He says that he'll try to put his desire for Silvia in check, but, if he can't, he'll use his "skill" to "compass" her. As a verb, "compass" can mean a few things. The editors of the 2008 *Norton Shakespeare* gloss this word to mean that Proteus intends to "win" Silvia. But, "compass" can also mean to "to seize" and it can also mean "to encircle, or surround something" (*Oxford English Dictionary*). In other words, it seems like Proteus's intention to "compass" Silvia is a lot more aggressive than a simple desire to "win" her heart. Keep reading….

PROTEUS
Sir Proteus, gentle lady, and your servant.
SILVIA
What's your will?
PROTEUS
That I may compass yours. (4.2.9)

Thought: Here's that word "compass" again. At 2.4.18 (above), Proteus used the term to suggest that he would use his "skill" to "compass" (win, seize, attain) Silvia. Here, his use of the word is even more tricky. On the one hand, Proteus suggests that he wants to "compass" (win) Silvia's *good* "will." (He wants to win her affection.) On the other hand, Proteus could also be suggesting that he intends to "compass" Silvia's *free* "will." This latter meaning seems to anticipate his attempt to rape Silvia, which is an act that aims to deprive her of all free choice and free will.

Come, I must bring you to our captain's cave:
Fear not; he bears an honourable mind,
And will not use a woman lawlessly. (5.3.3)

Thought: When the outlaws take Silvia captive, the First Outlaw promises that his "captain" will not assault her. This speaks to the fact that Valentine (the outlaws' "captain") isn't the kind of guy who goes around raping women (unlike Proteus). It also speaks to the fact that the forest is a pretty dangerous place for women – otherwise, why would the First Outlaw go out of his way to put Silvia's potential fears to rest?

Here can I sit alone, unseen of any,
And to the nightingale's complaining notes
Tune my distresses and record my woes.
O thou that dost inhabit in my breast,
Leave not the mansion so long tenantless,
Lest, growing ruinous, the building fall
And leave no memory of what it was!
Repair me with thy presence, Silvia; (5.4.1)

Thought: When Valentine gets kicked out of Milan for trying to elope with the Duke's daughter, he bums around a forest, where he finds a sense of peace bemoaning his sadness in harmony with the mournful sounds of the nightingale. As literary scholar Jean Howard reminds us, Valentine's reference to the nightingale recalls the mythic story of Philomela, who was raped by Tereus and eventually transformed into a nightingale – whose sad tune mourned the loss of Philomela's virginity. OK, we know what you're thinking. What does the mythic story of Philomela's rape and transformation into a bird have to do with Valentine hanging out in the forest missing his girlfriend? Well, it can't be a coincidence that moments after Valentine mentions the nightingale, his pal Proteus tries to rape Silvia in the very same forest, can it? Keep reading…

PROTEUS
Nay, if the gentle spirit of moving words
Can no way change you to a milder form,
I'll woo you like a soldier, at arms' end,
And love you 'gainst the nature of love,--force ye.
SILVIA
O heaven!
PROTEUS
I'll force thee yield to my desire.
VALENTINE
Ruffian, let go that rude uncivil touch,
Thou friend of an ill fashion! (5.4.5)

Thought: When Silvia refuses to love Proteus, he says he'll take her by "force," which is another way of saying that's he's going to rape her. He never completes the assault, however, because Proteus steps in and puts a stop to it.

Literary scholar Jean Howard points out that if Proteus *had* raped Silvia, the play would have been transformed from a comedy into a tragedy. But, because Valentine stops Proteus, *Two Gentlemen of Verona* escapes the genre of tragedy by the skin of its teeth.

Thou common friend, that's without faith or love,
For such is a friend now; treacherous man!
Thou hast beguiled my hopes; nought but mine eye
Could have persuaded me: now I dare not say
I have one friend alive; thou wouldst disprove me.
Who should be trusted, when one's own right hand
Is perjured to the bosom? (5.4.4)

Thought: OK, when Valentine stops Proteus from assaulting Silvia, we're expecting him to say something different here, right? But, instead of being angry that Proteus was going to violate *Silvia,* Valentine lectures Proteus about being a disloyal friend. What's going on here?

My shame and guilt confounds me.
Forgive me, Valentine: if hearty sorrow
Be a sufficient ransom for offence,
I tender 't here; I do as truly suffer
As e'er I did commit. (5.4.8)

Thought: After he's caught trying to rape Silvia, Proteus apologizes to Valentine, but not for his crime against Julia. Here, he apologizes for being a lousy friend to his guy pal, as if trying to rape Valentine's girlfriend was a crime against Valentine, and not Silvia.

Lies and Deceit Quotes

How angerly I taught my brow to frown,
When inward joy enforced my heart to smile! (1.2.18)

Thought: Julia admits that when she learned how Proteus had written her a letter, she was jumping for joy on the inside. But, she disguised her true feelings by pretending to be angry at his forwardness. In the first scene especially, Julia tends to play a lot of mind games when it comes to romance.

VALENTINE
I mean that her beauty is exquisite, but her favour infinite.
SPEED
That's because the one is painted and the other out
of all count. (2.1.15)

Thought: Here, Speed makes a nasty little jab at the practice of wearing makeup, which he perceives as a deceptive practice. According to Speed, the only reason Silvia looks like a "beauty" is because she covers her face with a "painted" mask.

We see this same kind of attitude toward women and cosmetics in plays like *Hamlet*, where, for example, King Claudius compares his "painted word[s]" (every lie he tells) to the way a "harlot" "plasters" her face with makeup:

The harlot's cheek, beautied with plastering art,
Is not more ugly to the thing that helps it
Than is my deed to my most painted word: (3.1.4)

VALENTINE
What means your ladyship? do you not like it?
SILVIA
Yes, yes; the lines are very quaintly writ;
But since unwillingly, take them again.
Nay, take them.
VALENTINE
Madam, they are for you.
SILVIA
Ay, ay: you writ them, sir, at my request;
But I will none of them; they are for you;
I would have had them writ more movingly. (2.1.33)

Thought: Julia isn't the only female character to play coy when it comes to romance. Here, Silvia becomes angry at Valentine for failing to realize that she wanted him to write her a love letter. The thing is, it's Silvia's own fault because, instead of just coming out and saying that she wanted a love note, she asked poor Valentine to write a letter to a "friend" of hers. We shouldn't be too hard on Silvia, though. After all, once she and Valentine are (secretly) engaged, she's incredibly loyal to him.

Now presently I'll give her father notice
Of their disguising and pretended flight;
Who, all enraged, will banish Valentine;

For Thurio, he intends, shall wed his daughter;
but, Valentine being gone, I'll quickly cross
By some sly trick blunt Thurio's dull proceeding.
Love, lend me wings to make my purpose swift,
As thou hast lent me wit to plot this drift! (2.6.1)

Thought: When Valentine and Silvia fall in love, they get engaged in secret and hatch a plan to elope. (Silvia's dad wants her to marry Thurio.) Pretty sneaky, right? But what's worse – the couples' plan to run off and marry in secret, or Proteus's plan to tattle on them to Silvia's father? Here, Proteus tells us that he's going to tell because he wants to steal Silvia away from both Thurio and his best friend, Valentine.

This love of theirs myself have often seen,
Haply when they have judged me fast asleep,
And oftentimes have purposed to forbid
Sir Valentine her company and my court: (3.1.2)

Thought: Huh. The Duke of Milan isn't as dumb as some characters seem to think. Here, he admits that he's suspected all along that Silvia and Valentine have been sneaking around behind his back.

Thy letters may be here, though thou art hence;
Which, being writ to me, shall be deliver'd
Even in the milk-white bosom of thy love.
The time now serves not to expostulate:
Come, I'll convey thee through the city-gate; (3.1.16)

Thought: That Proteus sure is tricky, isn't he? While he pretends to be heartbroken about his friend getting banished from Milan, he's actually planning to steal Silvia from Valentine. Here, he generously offers to escort Valentine to the city limits. How thoughtful.

The best way is to slander Valentine
With falsehood, cowardice and poor descent,
Three things that women highly hold in hate. (3.2.7)

Thought: We knew Proteus was bad before, but his deception just keeps getting worse. By this point, he's already arranged to get Valentine kicked out of Milan. Now, he's planning on talking trash about him to Silvia so she'll think he's a loser.

How many women would do such a message?
Alas, poor Proteus! thou hast entertain'd
A fox to be the shepherd of thy lambs.
Alas, poor fool! why do I pity him
[...]
And now am I, unhappy messenger,
To plead for that which I would not obtain,
To carry that which I would have refused,
To praise his faith which I would have dispraised.
I am my master's true-confirmed love;
But cannot be true servant to my master,
Unless I prove false traitor to myself.
Yet will I woo for him, but yet so coldly
As, heaven it knows, I would not have him speed. (4.4.6)

Thought: Poor Julia. When Proteus asks "Sebastian" (Julia in disguise) to deliver her ring to another woman, she actually feels bad that she's deceiving Proteus by being in disguise. Then she comes to her senses (sort of) when she recognizes that he really doesn't deserve her "pity." In the end, Julia completes the errand but acknowledges that, by playing the part of the obedient "servant" (she's been hired as Proteus's page boy), she's being a "traitor" to herself.

When all our pageants of delight were play'd,
Our youth got me to play the woman's part,
And I was trimm'd in Madam Julia's gown,
Which served me as fit, by all men's judgments,
As if the garment had been made for me:
Therefore I know she is about my height.
And at that time I made her weep agood,
For I did play a lamentable part:
Madam, 'twas Ariadne passioning
For Theseus' perjury and unjust flight;
Which I so lively acted with my tears
That my poor mistress, moved therewithal,
Wept bitterly; and would I might be dead
If I in thought felt not her very sorrow! (4.4.18)

Thought: The only way Julia can talk about her heartache is by pretending to be someone else. Here, she's disguised as "Sebastian" and she tells Silvia that she once borrowed Julia's clothes to plat the role of "Ariadne" in a church play. She goes on to fib that her performance of this "woman's part" was so good that it moved Julia to tears. "Ariadne" is a figure from Greek mythology – she's famous for hanging herself after her boyfriend, Theseus, breaks up with her. Now, we know that Julia/Sebastian never played the role of Ariadne in a play. This made up

story is Julia's only way of expressing her sadness over the loss of Proteus.

O Proteus, let this habit make thee blush!
Be thou ashamed that I have took upon me
Such an immodest raiment, if shame live
In a disguise of love:
It is the lesser blot, modesty finds,
Women to change their shapes than men their minds. (5.4.7)

Thought: When Julia reveals her true identity to Proteus, she declares that his cheating and infidelity are the worst kind of betrayal – worse than her own deception when she let him believe she was a boy ("Sebastian").

Gender Quotes

Thou, Julia, thou hast metamorphosed me,
Made me neglect my studies, lose my time,
War with good counsel, set the world at nought;
Made wit with musing weak, heart sick with thought. (1.1.11)

Thought: From the play's beginning, it seems that male-female relationships are never any good. Here, Proteus says that his love for Julia has transformed him, and not in a positive way.

What a fool is she, that knows I am a maid,
And would not force the letter to my view!
Since maids, in modesty, say 'no' to that
Which they would have the profferer construe 'ay.' (1.2.18)

Thought: After Julia refuses Proteus's letter, she reasons that it would be immodest and improper of her to accept the love note. While Julia worries a lot about what's considered proper or improper behavior for a young woman, she will later throw caution to the wind by disguising herself as a boy and travelling to Milan to find Proteus.

He wonder'd that your lordship
Would suffer him to spend his youth at home,
While other men, of slender reputation,
Put forth their sons to seek preferment out:
Some to the wars, to try their fortune there;
Some to discover islands far away;
Some to the studious universities.

For any or for all these exercises,
He said that Proteus your son was meet,
And did request me to importune you
To let him spend his time no more at home,
Which would be great impeachment to his age,
In having known no travel in his youth. (1.3.2)

Thought: Panthino advises Antonio that he should send Proteus to travel abroad like all the other young men from noble families. The idea is that travel will help round off a young man's education and make him a better person. This, of course, applies only to young *men*. Keep reading....

LUCETTA
Madam,
Dinner is ready, and your father stays. (1.2.18)

Thought: In the previous passage, we saw how young noblemen are expected to travel the world in order to become well-rounded individuals. This theory does not apply to young women, who are expected to remain at home. When Lucetta informs Julia that her father has called her to dinner, this becomes even more apparent – Julia is called to the table while Proteus is sent abroad. But, Julia doesn't just sit around the house in the play. As we know, she dons a disguise and travels to Milan, which is a pretty gutsy thing for her to do.

VALENTINE
I mean that her beauty is exquisite, but her favour infinite.
SPEED
That's because the one is painted and the other out
of all count. (2.1.15)

Thought: According to Speed, the only reason Silvia looks like a "beauty" is because she covers her face with a "painted" mask. Speed's nasty little jab at women who wear makeup seems to suggest that all women who wear cosmetics are deceitful. The thing is, however, Silvia is most definitely not a deceitful woman. (Unless we count the part where she plans to elope with Valentine.) In fact, she remains loyal and true to Valentine throughout the play, despite Proteus's attempts to lure her away.

Brain Snack: We see Speed's attitude toward women and cosmetics in other plays like *Hamlet*, where, for example, King Claudius compares his "painted word[s]" (every lie he tells) to the way a "harlot" "plasters" her face with makeup:

The harlot's cheek, beautied with plastering art,

Is not more ugly to the thing that helps it
Than is my deed to my most painted word: (3.1.4)

Sir Valentine, my friend,
This night intends to steal away your daughter:
Myself am one made privy to the plot.
I know you have determined to bestow her
On Thurio, whom your gentle daughter hates;
And should she thus be stol'n away from you,
It would be much vexation to your age. (3.1.1)

Thought: When Proteus tattles to the Duke that Silvia and Valentine plan to elope, he uses the language of theft to get Silvia's dad riled up. Valentine, he says, is going to "steal" the Duke's daughter, which suggests that young women are their fathers' possessions. We see also this kind of attitude in plays like *Othello*, where Iago tells Brabantio that he has been "robb'd" by a thief after Othello and Desdemona (Brabantio's daughter) elope (*Othello*, 1.1.7).

SPEED
'Item: She is slow in words.'
LANCE
O villain, that set this down among her vices! To
be slow in words is a woman's only virtue: I pray
thee, out with't, and place it for her chief virtue. (3.1.19)

Thought: When Speed helps Lance compose a list of Lance's girlfriend's virtues and vices, they argue about whether or not her "slowness in words" should be listed as a "vice" or a "virtue." This joke revolves around a common sixteenth-century belief – the so-called ideal woman was supposed to be virtuous, obedient, and *silent*.

JULIA
Madam, he sends your ladyship this ring.
SILVIA
The more shame for him that he sends it me;
For I have heard him say a thousand times
His Julia gave it him at his departure.
Though his false finger have profaned the ring,
Mine shall not do his Julia so much wrong.
JULIA
She thanks you. (4.4.4)

Thought: Here, Silvia refuses to accept the ring Proteus has sent her (by way of Julia, who is disguised as a page boy, "Sebastian"). Silvia insists that she would never do "Julia so much wrong," which gestures at Silvia's capacity for loyalty and solidarity with another woman (unlike Proteus, who is busy stabbing his best friend in the back).

Why, this it is to be a peevish girl,
That flies her fortune when it follows her.
I'll after, more to be revenged on Eglamour
Than for the love of reckless Silvia. (5.3.13)

Thought: Hmm. Apparently, Thurio isn't attracted to Silvia's free spirit and willful nature. Here, he decides that her "peevish" nature prevents her from being wife material.

All that was mine in Silvia I give thee. (5.4.5)

Thought: Did Valentine just say what we think he said? For a lot of readers and literary critics, this line means that Valentine is offering to "give" Silvia to his friend (who just tried to rape her) as a peace offering that will secure Valentine's friendship with Proteus.

Some critics, however, have read the lines a bit differently and argue that Shakespeare is trying to reconcile the tension between male friendship and male-female romance. For these critics, Valentine means to say something like "all the love I feel for Silvia, I give to thee, too." In other words, Valentine could be saying that he will love his friend and girlfriend equally.

When it comes down to it, the lines are pretty ambiguous. If we were hoping for Proteus's response to Valentine's offer to clear up the meaning for us, we're out of luck, because Proteus never responds to this line – that's because Julia/Sebastian faints and turns everybody's attention elsewhere.

What is in Silvia's face, but I may spy
More fresh in Julia's with a constant eye? (5.4.14)

Thought: Here, Proteus reveals that he's fallen back in love with Julia, who is still disguised as "Sebastian." For some readers, Proteus's renewed attraction to Julia raises questions about what it is, exactly, that Proteus is attracted to. He obviously recognizes Julia through the disguise, but it's not clear if Proteus is attracted to her because she looks like Julia, or because she looks like a boy. This moment also reminds us of the fact that the name "Sebastian" is commonly associated with male homoeroticism (as it is in *Twelfth Night*). Compare this passage to the <u>ending of *Twelfth Night*</u>, where Duke Orsino proposes to Viola (who is still wearing her "Cesario" disguise).

Marriage Quotes

O, that our fathers would applaud our loves,
To seal our happiness with their consents!
O heavenly Julia! (1.3.6)

Thought: When Proteus complains that he and Julia can't wed without their fathers' permission, we're alerted to the fact that fathers are the ones who stand in the way of their children's happiness in the world of the play. This has major implications for Valentine and Silvia, who try to elope because Silvia's father wants her to marry Thurio.

A woman sometimes scorns what best contents her.
Send her another; never give her o'er;
For scorn at first makes after-love the more.
If she do frown, 'tis not in hate of you,
But rather to beget more love in you:
If she do chide, 'tis not to have you gone;
For why, the fools are mad, if left alone.
Take no repulse, whatever she doth say;
For 'get you gone,' she doth not mean 'away!'
Flatter and praise, commend, extol their graces;
Though ne'er so black, say they have angels' faces.
That man that hath a tongue, I say, is no man,
If with his tongue he cannot win a woman. (3.1.6)

Thought: According to Valentine, the only way for a man to "win a woman" is by using his tongue to flatter and woo her. On the one hand, this seems to be a condemnation of Proteus's tactics (resorting to rape when a woman refuses his advances). At the same time, however, Valentine is also insistent that if a woman is unresponsive to a man's overtures, she's just playing games. He says that if a woman tells a guy to get lost, she doesn't really mean it. This kind of attitude toward "winning" a woman is pretty dangerous, don't you think? We wonder if Valentine's advice is really that different from Proteus's approach, which is also to disregard the wishes of the woman he wants.

I now am full resolved to take a wife
And turn her out to who will take her in:
Then let her beauty be her wedding-dower;
For me and my possessions she esteems not. (3.1.7)

Thought: This is a strange moment in the play. Here, the unmarried Duke tells Valentine that he's decided to "take a wife," which means that he's ready to boot Silvia out of the house without a "wedding-dower" (because she's a disrespectful daughter). Is the Duke just trying to scare off Valentine? Maybe he's hoping Valentine will lose interest in Silvia if he thinks she has no dowry? If so, why doesn't the Duke just say that he's going to kick Silvia out of the house? What does his so-called interest in finding a new wife have to do with his daughter living at home?

What's here?
'Silvia, this night I will enfranchise thee.'
'Tis so; and here's the ladder for the purpose. (3.1.18)

Thought: Uh-oh. Valentine is totally busted when the Duke finds a love letter to Silvia in Valentine's coat. When a rope ladder falls out of Valentine's jacket, it's also pretty clear that Valentine is planning on pulling a "Romeo and Juliet" maneuver by climbing up to Silvia's window and then eloping with the Duke's daughter. Like Romeo, Valentine is banished from the city limits and the love of his life when the Duke catches him. Good thing *Two Gentlemen of Verona* is a comedy and not a tragedy – comedies always end in marriage, so it's a pretty safe bet that things will work out for Silvia and Valentine.

She hath more qualities than a water-spaniel;
which is much in a bare Christian.

Pulling out a paper

Here is the cate-log of her condition.
'Imprimis: She can fetch and carry.' Why, a horse
can do no more: nay, a horse cannot fetch, but only
carry; therefore is she better than a jade. 'Item:
She can milk;' look you, a sweet virtue in a maid
with clean hands. (3.1.6)

Thought: When Lance announces that he's fallen in love with an unnamed woman, he proceeds to make a list of all her best features. It's pretty clear that Lance is interested in qualities that would make for a good wife, which, in Lance's mind, seems to be nothing more than a servant. It also seems like Shakespeare is using Lance to parody and make fun of the way the men (especially Thurio) in the play view love and marriage.

Thou art not ignorant what dear good will
I bear unto the banish'd Valentine,
Nor how my father would enforce me marry
Vain Thurio, whom my very soul abhors.
Thyself hast loved; and I have heard thee say
No grief did ever come so near thy heart
As when thy lady and thy true love died,
Upon whose grave thou vow'dst pure chastity. (4.3.3)

Thought: Here, Silvia asks her good friend Eglamour to help her run away and find Valentine. When Silvia explains why she's chosen to ask Eglamour for help, she reveals something interesting about his past. Eglamour, it seems, was married once and is now a widower. Not only that, but he loved his late wife so much that, since her death, he's sworn off all other women. It seems like Eglamour is one of the most loyal men in the play, which makes him a foil to the unfaithful Proteus.

O Proteus, let this habit make thee blush!
Be thou ashamed that I have took upon me
Such an immodest raiment, if shame live
In a disguise of love:
It is the lesser blot, modesty finds,
Women to change their shapes than men their minds. (5.4.7)

Thought: Although Julia is ashamed that she cross-dressed in order travel to Proteus, she says here that Proteus's behavior is even worse because his deception involved infidelity, which could have prevented their union in marriage. Julia's deception and social impropriety, on the hand, is excusable and justifiable because cross-dressing as "Sebastian" enabled her to reunite with Proteus and ensure a wedding match.

What's the big deal about Julia disguising herself as a boy, you ask? Well, sixteenth-century Puritans thought cross-dressing (especially on stage) was a major sin. Check out Phillip Stubbes's anti-theater rant in a book called *The Anatomy of Abuses* (1583): "Our apparel was given as a sign distinctive, to discern betwixt sex and sex, and therefore one to wear the apparel of another sex, is…to adulterate the verity of his own kind…these women [who cross-dress] may not improperly be called *Hermaphroditi*, that is Monsters of both kinds, half women, half men." So, this sort of explains why Julia has been feeling so ashamed of her disguise.

VALENTINE
Come, come, a hand from either:
Let me be blest to make this happy close;

'Twere pity two such friends should be long foes.
PROTEUS
Bear witness, Heaven, I have my wish for ever.
JULIA
And I mine. (5.4.7)

Thought: We know what you're thinking. Why the heck does Julia take Proteus back (and agree to marry him) about two seconds after Proteus tries to rape Silvia? We're wondering the same thing ourselves. Some critics see this as evidence that *Two Gentlemen* is a lousy play – the reunion between Julia and Proteus is completely unrealistic. Other critics point out that the engagement may be abrupt and strange to us but "comedy" always ends in marriage so, we shouldn't be so surprised. So, what do *you* think about all this?

DUKE
Thou art a gentleman and well derived;
Take thou thy Silvia, for thou hast deserved her.
VALENTINE
I thank your grace; the gift hath made me happy.
I now beseech you, for your daughter's sake,
To grant one boom that I shall ask of you. (5.4.1)

Thought: In the play, it's Silvia's father who determines the conditions of her wedding. When Thurio announces that he doesn't want to marry Silvia, the Duke immediately offers Silvia to Valentine because he has earned ("deserved") her, as if the Duke's daughter is a possession that he can bestow on the man of his choosing. We also notice that Valentine responds to the offer in the same terms – he thanks the Duke for the generous "gift" (that would be Silvia).

Come Proteus [...]
our day of marriage shall be yours;
One feast, one house, one mutual happiness. (5.4.14)

Thought: Here, Valentine tells Proteus they should all celebrate by have a *double* wedding. This is pretty typical of Shakespearean comedy, which always ends in marriage. Does this mean that Valentine's bromance with Proteus is being replaced by his marriage to Silvia? Not necessarily. Valentine says the double wedding will be "one feast, one house, one mutual happiness."

This whole "mutual happiness" comment seems to play on the biblical idea that, when a man and woman marry, they become united as "one flesh" (Genesis 2.24). The funny thing is, Valentine isn't talking to his future wife here. He's speaking *to Proteus*. What's up with that? Does Valentine mean that Proteus will enjoy "one mutual happiness" with his bride-to-be? Does he suggest that Valentine and Proteus will share "one mutual happiness"? Is Valentine saying

that both couples will enjoy "one mutual happiness"? Something else?

These final lines are pretty tricky. How we interpret them is likely to determine how we interpret the entire play – does Valentine's final speech resolve all of the tension between male friendship and male-female romance that we've seen throughout the play? Or does it just raise even more questions about which kind of relationship is more important?

Society and Class Quotes

LUCETTA
What would your ladyship?
JULIA
Is't near dinner-time?
LUCETTA
I would it were,
That you might kill your stomach on your meat
And not upon your maid. (1.2.4)

Thought: Here, Lucetta suggests that she wishes Julia would expend some of her energy by eating dinner. That way, Julia would be less likely to take out her rage and anger on her woman in waiting. As Julia's servant, there's little Lucetta can do when Julia throws a tantrum. It seems like Lucetta's only option is to tease and mock Julia when she behaves badly.

PANTHINO
He wonder'd that your lordship
Would suffer him to spend his youth at home,
While other men, of slender reputation,
Put forth their sons to seek preferment out:
Some to the wars, to try their fortune there;
Some to discover islands far away;
Some to the studious universities.
For any or for all these exercises,
He said that Proteus your son was meet,
And did request me to importune you
To let him spend his time no more at home,
Which would be great impeachment to his age,
In having known no travel in his youth. (1.3.2)

Thought: It doesn't take much for Panthino to convince Antonio that Proteus should travel to Milan. That's because Proteus's father is concerned about what other noblemen think of him. He's also concerned about making sure that his son does everything that a young nobleman is supposed to do – like travel abroad to see the world.

VALENTINE
Ha! let me see: ay, give it me, it's mine:
Sweet ornament that decks a thing divine!
Ah, Silvia, Silvia!
SPEED
Madam Silvia! Madam Silvia!
VALENTINE
How now, sirrah?
SPEED
She is not within hearing, sir.
VALENTINE
Why, sir, who bade you call her?
SPEED
Your worship, sir; or else I mistook.
VALENTINE
Well, you'll still be too forward. (2.1.2)

Thought: In the play, much of the clever back-and-forth dialogue is characterized by Speed out-witting his master. Here, Speed insults Valentine's love interest and gets away with it.

VALENTINE
What should I see then?
SPEED
Your own present folly and her passing deformity:
for he, being in love, could not see to garter his
hose, and you, being in love, cannot see to put on your hose.
VALENTINE
Belike, boy, then, you are in love; for last
morning you could not see to wipe my shoes.
SPEED
True, sir; I was in love with my bed: I thank you,
you swinged me for my love, which makes me the
bolder to chide you for yours. (2.1.22)

Thought: When Speed mocks his master for being blinded by love, Valentine responds by trying to put Speed back in his place. By reminding his servant that he roused him out of bed that morning to polish his shoes, Valentine lets Speed know who's boss.

SPEED
O jest unseen, inscrutable, invisible,
As a nose on a man's face, or a weathercock on a steeple!
My master sues to her, and she hath
taught her suitor,
He being her pupil, to become her tutor.
O excellent device! was there ever heard a better,
That my master, being scribe, to himself should write
the letter? (2.1.31)

Thought: Speed may be a servant but he's pretty sharp. When Silvia tricks Valentine into writing her a love letter, Valentine doesn't understand what's going on – Speed has to point it out to him.

I think Crab, my dog, be the sourest-natured
dog that lives: my mother weeping, my father
wailing, my sister crying, our maid howling, our cat
wringing her hands, and all our house in a great
perplexity, yet did not this cruel-hearted cur shed
one tear: (2.3.1)

Thought: It seems like the servants in the play often function as foils to the main characters. Here, Lance's relationship with his beloved dog Crab is a parody of some of the romantic relationships in the play. Like Julia, Lance is completely loyal and devoted to his pooch.

I am but a fool, look you; and yet I have the wit to
think my master is a kind of a knave: but that's
all one, if he be but one knave. He lives not now
that knows me to be in love; (3.1.6)

Thought: Lance takes a lot of pleasure in the fact that he keeps secrets from his master. Here, he calls Proteus a "knave" (an idiot) and reveals that he's fallen in love with an unnamed woman.

Third Outlaw
By the bare scalp of Robin Hood's fat friar,
This fellow were a king for our wild faction!
First Outlaw
We'll have him. Sirs, a word.
SPEED

Master, be one of them; it's an honourable kind of thievery. (4.1.5)

Thought: This reference to Robin Hood hints that the outlaws might be spending their time stealing from the rich and giving to the poor, especially when Speed says their crimes are an "honourable kind of thievery."

Second Outlaw
Tell us this: have you any thing to take to?
VALENTINE
Nothing but my fortune.
Third Outlaw
Know, then, that some of us are gentlemen,
Such as the fury of ungovern'd youth
Thrust from the company of awful men:
Myself was from Verona banished
For practising to steal away a lady,
An heir, and near allied unto the duke. (4.1.6)

Thought: The Third Outlaw goes out of his way to point out that the forest dwelling gang is made up of noblemen. What's up with that?

He thrusts me himself into the company of three or four
gentlemanlike dogs under the duke's table: he had
not been there--bless the mark!--a pissing while, but
all the chamber smelt him. 'Out with the dog!' says
one: 'What cur is that?' says another: 'Whip him
out' says the third: 'Hang him up' says the duke.
I, having been acquainted with the smell before,
knew it was Crab, and goes me to the fellow that
whips the dogs: 'Friend,' quoth I, 'you mean to whip
the dog?' 'Ay, marry, do I,' quoth he. 'You do him
the more wrong,' quoth I; ''twas I did the thing you
wot of.' He makes me no more ado, but whips me out
of the chamber. How many masters would do this for
his servant? (4.4.1)

Thought: As Lance recounts how he saved Crab from punishment for peeing under the Duke's table, we learn that Lance took a whipping for his dog. Though we don't see this violence on stage, it seems like much of the humor in the play revolves around Lance's stories about being physically abused by his social "betters." This anticipates the kind of slap-stick humor we see in Shakespeare's *The Comedy of Errors*, where the servants (the Dromio brothers) are always

being smacked around.

Plot Analysis

Study Questions

1. What does the play value more – male friendship or marriage? Does the play ever reconcile the tension between the two?
2. Why does Valentine forgive Proteus so quickly and easily after Proteus tries to rape Silvia in Act 5, Scene 4?
3. How does *Two Gentlemen of Verona* compare to Shakespeare's other "comedies" (like _A Midsummer Night's Dream_ , _As You Like It_, and _Twelfth Night_)? Does Shakespeare take ideas, themes, or conventions from *Two Gentlemen* and rework them in his later plays?
4. What's the function of the servants in *Two Gentlemen*? How do the antics of Lance and Speed create meaning in the play? Do they have any impact on the plot? What do they contribute?
5. "O heaven!" screams Silvia as Proteus tries to assault her (5.4.6). These two words are Silvia's last spoken lines in the play. She's silent while Valentine and Proteus make up, says nothing while Julia and Proteus get back together, and she watches silently as her father gives her as a "gift" to Proteus. If Silvia had a voice in the final moments of the play, what do you think she might have to say?

Characters

All Characters

Proteus Character Analysis

Proteus is a young nobleman from Verona. He's *supposed* to be Valentine's best friend and Julia's sweetie, but after he falls for Valentine's girlfriend, he stabs his BFF in the back and tries to rape Silvia. When he's confronted, he undergoes a sudden and miraculous

transformation, which prompts him to make up with Valentine and fall back in love with Julia.

Like the shape-shifting sea god he shares his name with, Proteus is pretty erratic and changeable, don't you think? He falls in and out of love (with women and his best friend) as often as some people change clothes, and he's also pretty crafty and deceptive. He has no trouble being two-faced as he betrays his best friend and he lies to just about everyone he knows.

Male Friendship
OK, Proteus sounds like a pretty bad guy. So why is his horrible behavior forgiven at the play's end? Well, we're not quite sure – the sequence of events in the final scene is pretty bizarre. Still, we can try to understand why Valentine and Julia forgive Proteus by thinking about the play's themes of male friendship and transformation.

First things first. Let's think about the importance of male friendship in the play. At the beginning of *Two Gentlemen*, Proteus and Valentine are best buds. Check out how sweet Proteus is when Valentine sets out for Milan: "Wilt thou be gone? Sweet Valentine, adieu!/ Think on thy Proteus" when you're away (1.1.1). It's pretty clear that Valentine also feels the same way about his BFF. When the Duke of Milan asks about Proteus's character, Valentine says, "I know him as myself; for from our infancy/ We have conversed and spent our hours together" (2.4.20). According to Valentine, the guys have known each other since they were babies and have spent their entire lives together. When Proteus says, "I know him as myself," he means to suggest that he knows Proteus *as well as* he knows himself. At the same time, the phrase "I know him *as myself*" also suggests that Proteus and Valentine are like two halves of the same being.

This idea echoes a common sixteenth-century idea made famous by Thomas Elyot's *The Book Named the Governor*. In Book 2, Chapter 11, Elyot says that friendship makes "two persons one in having and suffering. And therefore a friend is properly named of philosophers the other I. For that in them is but one mind and one possession" (2.11). In Shakespeare's day, male friendship was considered one of the most sacred and important bonds.

So, when Valentine catches Proteus trying to rape Silvia, Valentine is outraged that his friend would betray him. For Valentine, Proteus's violation of Silvia is less important than Proteus's violation of the bonds of friendship. When Proteus apologizes, he says he's sorry for being a bad friend, *not* for the attempted rape:

My shame and guilt confounds me.
Forgive me, Valentine: if hearty sorrow
Be a sufficient ransom for offence,
I tender 't here; I do as truly suffer
As e'er I did commit. (5.4.4)

Proteus never expresses remorse for his crime against Silvia. He feels bad because he hurt Valentine's feelings and betrayed his friend's trust. When Valentine forgives him without a lot of fuss, the play seems to suggest that mending male friendship is more important than anything else.

Proteus's Final Transformation?

OK, so we can begin to understand Valentine's motivation to forgive Proteus, but why does Julia forgive him? There are no easy answers to this question, but, again, we try to understand by taking a close look at the play. Here's what Julia says after Proteus assaults Silvia:

O Proteus, let this habit make thee blush!
Be thou ashamed that I have took upon me
Such an immodest raiment, if shame live
In a disguise of love:
It is the lesser blot, modesty finds,
Women to change their shapes than men their minds. (5.4.7)

Again, there's no mention of Silvia. Julia is irate because 1) she's embarrassed that she had to dress as a boy ("Sebastian") in order to chase down Proteus, and 2) because Proteus has been unfaithful and "change[d]" his mind about loving her. How does Proteus respond to this?

Than men their minds! 'tis true.
O heaven! were man
But constant, he were perfect. (5.4.7)

Here, Proteus suddenly realizes that Julia is right about his behavior – he's been falling in and out of love and his disloyalty and inconstancy makes him flawed. (Yet, there's still no recognition that his attempt to rape Silvia is problematic.) What's going on here? Literary scholar Marjorie Garber points out that, at this moment in the play, Proteus's true nature is "unmasked" at the exact same time that Julia's true identity has been revealed (*Shakespeare After All*, 46). The point may be that, while human beings can be fickle, changeable, and unstable, they are also capable of self-revelation and change (for the better). At the same time, the abruptness of Proteus's seeming transformation leaves us skeptical at best.

Check out "What's Up With the Ending?" if you want to think about this some more.

Proteus Timeline and Summary

- 1.1: Proteus says an emotional goodbye to Valentine and explains why he's staying behind in Verona while his buddy goes off to see the world – Proteus is in love with Julia and can't stand to be away from her. Proteus then asks Speed if his love letter was

delivered to Julia.

- 2.2: The next time we see Proteus, he's saying an emotional goodbye to Julia. (Proteus's dad has decided to send him to Milan, where Valentine is.) Proteus exchanges rings with Julia and promises to be faithful.

- 2.4: Proteus arrives at the Duke's court in Milan, greets his best bud, takes one look at Silvia, and then falls in love with his best friend's girlfriend. Left alone on stage, Proteus tells us he's fallen out of love with Julia and his BFF, Valentine. He'll try to stop himself from being in love with Silvia, but, if he can't, he'll do anything he can to win her.

- 2.6: Proteus gives us a big speech about how he's torn between Valentine and Silvia. Then he announces he's going to get his friend out of the picture by telling Silvia's dad that Valentine plans to elope with his daughter.

- 3.1: Proteus makes good on his promise and tattles on Valentine so he'll get booted out of the court. After Valentine gets banished, Proteus pretends to be a loving and concerned friend and then escorts Valentine to the city limits.

- 3.2: With Valentine out of the way, Proteus now schemes to win Silvia's heart and get Thurio out of the way. Proteus comes up with the idea to talk trash about Valentine to Silvia.

- 4.2: Proteus pretends to be Thurio's friend and acts like he's going to help him get Silvia. They go to Julia's window and serenade her. When Thurio goes home, Proteus makes his move and gets rejected by Silvia.

- 4.4: Some time between Act 4, Scene 2 and Act 4, Scene 4, Proteus sends Lance to give Silvia a gift – a little lap dog. Here, Proteus learns that his gift never made it to Silvia (the little dog ran away). Proteus meets "Sebastian," who is really Julia. (She's come to see Proteus.) Proteus hires "Sebastian" and then sends "him" to deliver a ring to Silvia (the same ring Julia gave him!).

- 5.2: Proteus continues to pretend he's helping Thurio get Silvia and gives Thurio some bad advice. When the Duke arrives with news that he's going to the forest to find a runaway Silvia, Proteus announces he's going, too.

- 5.4: In the forest, Proteus has somehow caught up with Silvia. He tries, unsuccessfully, to convince her that she owes him for finding her. When Silvia tells him to scram, Proteus tries to rape her. Proteus is confronted by Valentine and apologizes for being a disloyal friend (he doesn't apologize for trying to assault Silvia). When Valentine offers to let Proteus have Silvia for himself, he doesn't have a chance to reply because "Sebastian" faints and then reveals that "he" is actually "Julia." Seeing Julia, Proteus falls back in love with her and gets engaged.

Valentine Character Analysis

The most important thing to know about Valentine is that he is Proteus's BFF. At least we're pretty sure that's what Valentine would want us to say. (If you haven't already read our analysis of Proteus, you should do that now because these guys are like two peas in a pod –

they're the Batman and Robin of sixteenth-century literature, the Han Solo and Chewbacca of Shakespearean comedy, the Captain Kirk and Spock of Renaissance drama. You catch our drift?)

Valentine and Romance

This young gentleman from Verona is guilty of some pretty bizarre behavior in the play – after catching his best friend trying to rape his girlfriend Silvia, he forgives Proteus and then offers to "give" Silvia over to Proteus as a gesture of friendship. We know you're just dying to know more about Valentine's oh-so generous offer to his friend, but first we need to think about Valentine's attitude toward love.

At the beginning of the play, Valentine seems like a hater – he mocks Proteus for being in love with Julia and claims that romance has transformed Proteus into a "fool" (1.1.8).

If haply won, perhaps a hapless gain;
If lost, why then a grievous labour won;
However, but a folly bought with wit,
Or else a wit by folly vanquished. (1.1.6)

According to Valentine, if a man succeeds in winning a woman's heart, it is a "hapless gain." On the other hand, if a man loses in love, it's a "labour won." Pretty cynical, don't you think?

Valentine Meets Silvia

Enter Silvia. When Valentine meets the Duke of Milan's sassy daughter, everything changes. He falls in love and proceeds to play the part of the male lover in a courtly romance. This basically means that Valentine places Silvia on a pedestal while Silvia treats Valentine like her "servant." (That's how guys and girls flirt in "courtly romance" literature like Chaucer's "The Knight's Tale." And yes, Shakespeare is totally making fun of courtly romance. Chaucer, by the way, made fun of it too. Just read "The Miller's Tale " if you don't believe us.)

Valentine is so smitten with Silvia that he literally risks his neck to be with her. When Silvia's dad banishes Valentine from Milan, Valentine gets pretty dramatic. Check out what he has to say in the play's most famous monologue:

To die is to be banish'd from myself;
And Silvia is myself: banish'd from her
Is self from self: a deadly banishment!
What light is light, if Silvia be not seen?
What joy is joy, if Silvia be not by? (3.1.15)

In elevated terms, Valentine declares that life is meaningless for him without Silvia, so much so that fleeing from Milan is as good as dying. Valentine seems like he's pretty crazy about Silvia, right? There's just one thing. His big speech about Silvia is way over the top. We might say that

it's a little *too* over the top. When Valentine elevates Silvia in an unrealistic way, we wonder if his love is really genuine.

Valentine's Offer to Proteus

Even if we question Valentine's devotion to Silvia, we're still pretty shocked when Valentine offers to "give" her over to his best friend, especially since Valentine's offer comes on the heels of Proteus's attempt to rape Silvia (5.4). Here's how it goes down:

After Proteus apologizes to Valentine for being a lousy friend (there's no apology for assaulting Silvia), Valentine forgives him immediately and says, "All that was mine in Silvia I give thee" (5.4.5). There are a few ways to read this:

1. Any claims I made to Silvia's love, I give thee. (He's going to step aside and let Proteus have her.)
2. All the love I gave to Silvia, I give thee. (He loves Proteus more than he loves Silvia.)
3. All the love I gave to Silvia, I'll give to you too. (He'll love Proteus and Silvia equally.)

Most literary critics tend to agree that Valentine is making a peace offering here, which implies that he values his friendship with Proteus more than any other relationship. Does this also mean that the play values friendship more than anything? We'll leave that for you to decide. Be sure to check out the "Theme" of "Friendship" if you want to think about this some more.

Valentine Timeline and Summary

- 1.1: After an emotional goodbye to Proteus, Valentine heads off to see the world…of Italy that is.
- 2.1 So much has happened since we last saw our boy. Valentine has landed at the Duke's court in Milan, where he has fallen in love with Silvia. At Silvia's request, Valentine has written a love letter to an unnamed "friend" of Silvia's. (That's Silvia's coy way of asking Valentine to write her a steamy love note.) Here, Valentine hands over the uninspired love letter (he has no idea it's supposed to be for Silvia) and gets in trouble with his girl. After Silvia storms off, Speed explains why she's mad.
- 2.4 Valentine flirts with Silvia in front of the guy (Thurio) to whom Silvia is supposed to be getting engaged. When the Duke arrives with news that Proteus is coming to town, Valentine makes a big speech about how awesome Proteus is. Proteus enters. He and Valentine brag about their girlfriends. Valentine confesses that he's secretly engaged to Silvia – they're planning to elope.
- 3.1 While he's on his way to sneak into Silvia's bedroom window, Valentine is confronted by Silvia's dad, the Duke, who banishes him. Valentine makes a big speech about how being away from Silvia is a fate worse than death. Valentine speaks with Proteus and then hightails it out of Milan.
- 4.1 In a forest between Milan and Mantua, Valentine is accosted by a band of outlaws, who

decide Valentine is cool enough to be their new leader. He agrees to live with his new friends in the forest.

- 5.4 Valentine misses Silvia, but he tells us that he doesn't miss the chaos of court. Valentine is in the middle of a big speech when he sees Proteus trying to rape Silvia in the woods. He stops the attempted rape and yells at Proteus for being a disloyal friend. (No word from him about rape being wrong.) When Proteus says he's sorry, Valentine offers to "give" Silvia to Proteus. When the Duke arrives, Valentine is given permission to wed Silvia. (Still no communication with Silvia, who is standing right beside him.) Valentine says there should be a double wedding – Proteus and Julia can get hitched at the same time Valentine marries Silvia.

Julia Character Analysis

Julia is a young noblewoman from Verona. In the play, she disguises herself as a boy and follows her boyfriend, Proteus, to Milan, where she catches him trying to hook up with another woman.

Julia and Love

At the beginning of the play, Julia seems like she's just as fickle as some of the other characters – she can't seem to make up her mind about whether or not she'll allow herself to fall in love, so she asks her serving woman, "But say, Lucetta, now we are alone,/ Wouldst thou then counsel me to fall in love?" (1.2.1). Just a few lines later, she wonders who should be the lucky guy: "Of all the fair resort of gentlemen/ That every day with parle encounter me,/ In thy opinion which is worthiest love?" (1.2.2). OK, Julia is obviously a very popular girl – she's got suitors coming out of the woodwork just to talk with her.

We soon find out that Julia's had her sights set on Proteus all along. Julia slyly asks Lucetta's opinion of Proteus and, when Lucetta suggests the guy's a clown, Julia is furious: "How now! what means this passion at his name?" (1.2.6). Julia's fickle behavior continues throughout the scene, where she works *really* hard to conceal her true feelings for Proteus (by sending back a love letter, changing her mind, and then proceeding to tear it up to prove that she doesn't care about love) (1.2). Julia's not the only character to behave strangely. Shakespeare's point seems to be that love makes us do strange things, especially when we try to conceal our feelings.

The thing about Julia, however, is that she turns out to be pretty steadfast in her devotion to her boyfriend, Proteus. After Proteus leaves for Milan, she's determined to be with him and risks everything (including potential unwanted encounters with "lascivious men") by traveling to Milan.

Shakespeare's First Cross-Dressing Heroine

Julia is also pretty clever. In order to travel safely, she disguises herself as a boy, "Sebastian."

This is pretty gutsy, don't you think? But then Julia doesn't something pretty strange when she arrives in Milan and catches Proteus hitting on Silvia. Instead of revealing her identity, she takes a job as Proteus's pageboy and then proceeds to run a painful errand – delivering a ring to Silvia on behalf of Proteus. Why would she do this? Is she a glutton for punishment? Is she hoping to size up the competition? We're not exactly sure but we do know this – Julia's not the only character to behave this way. In _Twelfth Night_, Viola falls in love with Duke Orsino after taking a job as his page boy (also named "Sebastian") and then agrees to delivers love letters to another woman, Olivia.

Julia's Encounter with Silvia

Julia's disguise is important for all sorts of reasons. First, it draws the audience's attention to the fact that we are watching (or reading) a play in which a male actor is playing the role of a woman who is disguised as a boy. (Women actors, as we know, weren't allowed on the Elizabethan stage, so the parts of women were played by men and boys.) Shakespeare has a lot of fun with Julia's "Sebastian" disguise. Check out what Julia says when Silvia asks "Sebastian" to tell her about Julia:

Our youth got me to play the woman's part,
And I was trimm'd in Madam Julia's gown,
Which served me as fit, by all men's judgments,
As if the garment had been made for me:
Therefore I know she is about my height.
And at that time I made her weep agood,
For I did play a lamentable part:
Madam, 'twas Ariadne passioning
For Theseus' perjury and unjust flight;
Which I so lively acted with my tears
That my poor mistress, moved therewithal,
Wept bitterly; and would I might be dead
If I in thought felt not her very sorrow! (4.4.18)

Shakespeare loves this kind of artistic self-reference – he's always letting us know that we're watching a play and he's always reminding us that the world of the stage is _not_ the real world in which we live. At the same time, when "Sebastian" relates the story of how "his" acting role made Julia "weep," we're reminded of the theater's capacity to move us. For Shakespeare, the theater can also be a reflection of the kinds of emotions we experience in the real world.

It's also interesting that "Sebastian" claims to have worn Julia's clothes when "he" played the role of Ariadne in a church play. "Sebastian's" performance of this "woman's part" was so good, "he" says, that it moved Julia to tears. Ariadne is a figure from Greek mythology. She's famous for hanging herself after her boyfriend, Theseus, breaks up with her. (Never a good idea.) Now, we know that "Sebastian" never played the role of Ariadne in a play. This made up story seems to be Julia's way of expressing her sadness over the loss of Proteus without

revealing her true identity, which is kind of touching.

Julia Timeline and Summary

- 1.2: Julia hangs out with Lucetta and contemplates whether or not she should fall in love and, if so, which one of her many boyfriends she should choose. Julia decides on Proteus. When Lucetta tries to give Julia a letter from Proteus, she refuses to read it and sends it back. Then she changes her mind and asks for the letter. When Lucetta teases her, Julia tears it to shreds and then tries to piece it back together.
- 2.2: Julia is told that Proteus must leave town and the two say a tearful goodbye.
- 2.7: Julia resolves to track down Proteus in Milan. She asks Lucetta to rustle up some pants because she's going to disguise herself as a boy (to avoid being raped while travelling alone).
- 4.2: Julia has arrived in Milan disguised as "Sebastian." As she's being led to the Duke's house, she sees Proteus hit on Silvia and she is devastated.
- 4.4: Julia (still disguised as "Sebastian"), takes a job as Proteus's pageboy and agrees to deliver a ring to Silvia on Proteus's behalf. Julia/Sebastian meets Silvia and makes up a story about how Sebastian was in a play and borrowed Julia's clothes because it was a woman's part.
- 5.4: Julia/Sebastian has accompanied Proteus and the Duke to the forest in search of Silvia. Julia witnesses Proteus's attempted rape of Silvia, Valentine's intervention, and Proteus and Valentine's big make-up scene. When Valentine offers to let Proteus have Silvia, Julia/Sebastian faints. When she comes to, she reveals her true identity and yells at Proteus. After Proteus declares he has fallen back in love with Julia, Julia joins hands with Proteus and gets engaged.

Silvia Character Analysis

Silvia is the spirited daughter of the Duke of Milan and Valentine's girlfriend. When she falls in love with Valentine, she rebels against her father's wishes and makes plans to elope. Silvia is so determined to be with Valentine that, when her father banishes Valentine from Milan, Silvia runs away to the forest, where Valentine has set up camp.

Silvia's Loyalty
Silvia is not only bold, she's also incredibly loyal, which is a pretty big deal in a play in which the two main characters (Proteus and Valentine, we're talking about you) are anything but. When Proteus stabs his best friend Valentine in the back and goes after Silvia, Silvia seems to be the only voice of morality and fidelity:

PROTEUS
In love
Who respects friend?
SILVIA
All men but Proteus. (5.4.5)

Silvia also demonstrates her capacity for kindness when she refuses to accept a gift from
Proteus:

The more shame for him that he sends it me;
For I have heard him say a thousand times
His Julia gave it him at his departure.
Though his false finger have profaned the ring,
Mine shall not do his Julia so much wrong. (4.4.4)

Silvia refuses to accept the ring Proteus has sent her (by way of Julia, who is disguised as a
page boy, "Sebastian"). She also insists that she would never do "Julia so much wrong," which
gestures at Silvia's capacity for loyalty and solidarity with another woman (unlike Proteus, who
is busy stabbing his best friend in the back). When we read this passage, we can't help but
think that, despite the play's efforts to champion the bonds of male friendship, Silvia's behavior
demonstrates how women are capable of friendship too.

What Happens to Silvia's Voice?
Silvia is definitely a strong heroine, but it seems like Shakespeare drops the ball in the play's
final scene. When Proteus threatens to rape her, Silvia screams "O heaven!" and this is the last
we hear from her (5.4.6). We're relieved when Valentine prevents the rape, but we're baffled
when Silvia remains silent on stage. When Valentine and Proteus make up, she says nothing.
When Julia and Proteus get back together, she's silent. When her father arrives and gives her
as a "gift" to Proteus, she says nothing. Is this a reflection of Shakespeare's inexperience as a
playwright? We're not sure. What do you think? We also wonder what Silvia might utter if she
did have a voice in the final moments of the play…

Silvia Timeline and Summary

- 2.4: At her dad's court in Milan, Silvia flirts with Valentine and mocks Thurio. When
  Proteus arrives, she greets him, engages in some witty banter, and then leaves.
- 4.2: Silvia is serenaded by Thurio and a band of musicians. She comes to her bedroom
  window after Thurio leaves and is hit on by Proteus, whom she rejects.
- 4.4: Silvia rejects the ring that "Sebastian" has been sent to deliver. She talks with
  "Sebastian" and asks about Julia.
- 5.1: Julia asks Eglamour to help her travel to the forest to find Valentine, who has been

banished.

- 5.3: In the forest, Silvia is captured by a band of outlaws who say they're going to take her to their friendly leader (Valentine).
- 5.4 Sometime between the last scene and now, Proteus has "rescued" Silvia from the outlaws. Proteus nearly rapes Silvia but Valentine prevents the attack. (We don't hear another word out of Silvia after this.) The Duke shows up and says Valentine can marry his daughter so, Silvia is engaged without having uttered a single word.

Speed Character Analysis

Speed is Valentine's clownish servant. He's got a quick wit and a habit of bagging on other characters in a way that reveals how foolish people can be. Check out what Speed says after Valentine brags about Silvia's beauty:

SPEED
You never saw her since she was deformed.
VALENTINE
How long hath she been deformed?
SPEED
Ever since you loved her.
VALENTINE
I have loved her ever since I saw her; and still I
see her beautiful.
SPEED
If you love her, you cannot see her.
VALENTINE
Why?
SPEED
Because Love is blind. O, that you had mine eyes;
or your own eyes had the lights they were wont to
have when you chid at Sir Proteus for going
ungartered! (2.1.18)

Obviously, Speed is pretty quick when it comes to clever dialogue. Instead of just coming out and saying to Valentine that love has blinded him, Speed engages his master in a dialogue that leads to him accusing Valentine of what amounts to wearing "love goggles." He also points out that it wasn't so long ago that Valentine was making fun of ("chid[ing]") Proteus for being in love with Julia.

Shakespeare's portrayal of Speed (and Lance) is relatively innovative. While servants in earlier sixteenth-century plays tended to mimic the behavior of their masters, Shakespeare does

something new in *Two Gentlemen.* In the play, Speed's attitude toward marriage and love calls attention to his master's flaws. This is a pretty big deal because Shakespeare is one of the first playwrights to portray servants who are capable of *defining* the main characters. Compare Speed's role in the play to that of Lance, whose devotion to Crab draws our attention to Proteus's disloyalty to Julia and Valentine.

We also want to point out that Speed's character anticipates some of Shakespeare more infamous clown figures, like Feste in *Twelfth Night*. (Like Speed, Feste also has penchant for accurately pointing out the folly of those around him – he points out that Olivia's excessive mourning is over-indulgent and "foolish" and notes Duke Orsino's extreme moodiness when he compares Orsino's mind to an "opal" that changes color.)

Lance Character Analysis

Lance ("Launce" in some editions of the play) is Proteus's servant. When Proteus is sent to Milan, Lance is forced to go along. He's reluctant to leave his beloved dog, Crab, behind and somehow manages to take the little guy along with him.

Lance often appears before the audience and delivers silly monologues about his relationship with his beloved Crab. Check out Lance's description of what happened when Crab got caught "a pissing" under the Duke's Table:

all the chamber smelt him. 'Out with the dog!' says
one: 'What cur is that?' says another: 'Whip him
out' says the third: 'Hang him up' says the duke.
I, having been acquainted with the smell before,
knew it was Crab, and goes me to the fellow that
whips the dogs: 'Friend,' quoth I, 'you mean to whip
the dog?' 'Ay, marry, do I,' quoth he. 'You do him
the more wrong,' quoth I; ''twas I did the thing you
wot of.' He makes me no more ado, but whips me out
of the chamber. How many masters would do this for
his servant? (4.4.1)

Lance is not only funny and entertaining, but he's also incredibly loyal to his dog. Rather than allow Crab to be whipped, Lance takes the blame *and* a beating for supposedly wetting his pants. We also learn that Lance has endured other punishments for Crab's bad behavior. He stood in the stocks when Crab stole some "puddings" and he stood on a pillory when Crab killed a neighbor's geese (4.4.1). It seems like Lance's relationship with Crab is a parody of some of the romantic relationships in the play, don't you think? Like the loyal Julia, who follows Proteus to the ends of the earth and forgives his infidelity, Lance is completely devoted to his pooch.

Crab Character Analysis

We thought you might come sniffing around here for an analysis of Lance's dog, Crab. We talk about him in "Symbols," which is where you should head now if you want to know what we think of him.

Duke of Milan Character Analysis

The Duke of Milan is Silvia's ridiculously over protective father. Seriously. He's the kind of guy who locks up his daughter at night so she can't sneak out: "I nightly lodge her in an upper tower,/ The key whereof myself have ever kept;/ And thence she cannot be conveyed away" (3.1.2). Yikes! Sounds like something out of a fairy tale, don't you think? When the Duke catches Valentine with a rope ladder and a steamy love note addressed to his daughter, he puts two and two together and does what any Shakespearean father would do – he flips out and banishes Silvia's boyfriend from his court, on pain of death: "Be gone. I will not hear thy vain excuse,/ but as thou lov'st thy life, make speed from hence" (3.1.18).

To some extent, the Duke is just as dangerous as Proteus in that he stands in the way of the lovers' happiness. His character also seems to anticipate the powerful Prince of Verona in _Romeo and Juliet_, who uses his clout to banish Romeo. In _Two Gentlemen of Verona_, the Duke is the guy who doles out all the punishment – this becomes even clearer when we learn that the forest-dwelling outlaws are former noblemen who have also been booted out of the Duke's court. At the same time, the Duke also seems to anticipate some of Shakespeare's other overbearing fathers. Like Juliet's dad, Lord Capulet, he's insistent that his daughter marry the man of his choosing and he threatens to throw his daughter out on the streets when she disobeys. After learning of Silvia's plans to elope, he declares that he's resolved to "turn her out" without a "wedding-dower" because she's so disrespectful and irreverent (3.1.7).

The Duke also tends to speak about his daughter as though she's a piece of property (_his_ property) that can be stolen away from him or bestowed upon another man. Check out this exchange between the Duke and Valentine in the play's final scene:

DUKE
[…] Sir Valentine,
Thou art a gentleman and well derived;
Take thou thy Silvia, for thou hast deserved her.
VALENTINE
I thank your grace; the gift hath made me happy. (5.4.1)

We see this kind of attitude in plays like _Taming of the Shrew_, where Baptista Minola arranges his daughters' marriages like a businessman, and in the tragedy of _Othello_, where Brabantio interprets his daughter's elopement with Othello as a kind of "theft" (_Othello_, 1.1).

Thurio Character Analysis

Thurio is a nobleman at the Duke's court in Milan. He's the Duke's favorite to marry Silvia, which makes him a rival to Valentine. Thurio is kind of arrogant and annoying, so he's not much competition for Valentine, even though he tries *really* hard to win Silvia. Like some of the other characters, Thurio is a tad bit fickle. He loses interest in Silvia as soon as she runs away to the forest to find Valentine:

Why, this it is to be a peevish girl,
That flies her fortune when it follows her.
I'll after, more to be revenged on Eglamour
Than for the love of reckless Silvia. (5.2.13)

We can understand why he doesn't want to be with a girl who is in love with another man, but, then again, the fact Silvia is in love with Valentine never seemed to stop him from pursuing her before. It seems like Thurio loses interest in Silvia because she's a disobedient daughter, which, in Thurio's mind, means that she'll also be a "disobedient" wife.

Thurio also seems a bit petty, especially when he says he's going to tag along with the Duke to the forest just so he can see Eglamour get in trouble for helping Silvia run away.

Lucetta Character Analysis

Lucetta is Julia's woman in waiting. She functions as a kind of sounding board for Julia, who confides in Lucetta and asks her for advice about romance and love:

JULIA
But say, Lucetta, now we are alone,
Wouldst thou then counsel me to fall in love?
LUCETTA
Ay, madam, so you stumble not unheedfully. (1.2. 1)

Lucetta seems to give pretty reasonable and grounded advice. Although she can be clever and sassy – she's not afraid to tease Julia about Proteus – we don't see much of her in the play. After she helps Julia disguise herself as a boy in Act 2, Scene 7, we never hear from her again.

Panthino Character Analysis

Panthino is Antonio's sensible servant. Like Lucetta, Panthino acts as a sounding board and dispenser of advice to his master, Antonio. In Act 1, Scene 3, Panthino advises Antonio to send Proteus abroad with all the other noblemen's sons:

'Twere good, I think, your lordship sent him thither:
There shall he practise tilts and tournaments,
Hear sweet discourse, converse with noblemen.
And be in eye of every exercise
Worthy his youth and nobleness of birth. (1.3.4)

Here, Panthino gives voice to the idea that young noblemen should travel abroad and hang out with other men of noble "birth" as a way to round out one's education. The question is, does Proteus actually learn anything in Milan?

After his conversation with Antonio, Panthino has a very small role in the play – namely, making sure Proteus and Lance catch their "ship" to Milan.

Eglamour Character Analysis

Eglamour is a gentleman at the Duke's court in Milan. We don't hear much from Eglamour, but Silvia describes him as "Valiant, wise, remorseful, well accomplish'd" (4.3.3). Because he knows a thing or two about love and heartache, he agrees to help Silvia run away from Milan to find Valentine. When Silvia asks for his help, she reveals Eglamour's back-story:

Thyself hast loved; and I have heard thee say
No grief did ever come so near thy heart
As when thy lady and thy true love died,
Upon whose grave thou vow'dst pure chastity. (4.3.3)

Eglamour sounds like a pretty loyal guy, don't you think? Apparently, when his "true love died," he vowed to remain celibate. (Notice how the Italian word for love appears in Egl*amour*'s name?) Now, he's being a great friend to Julia by agreeing to escort her to the forest. This makes Eglamour a perfect foil to Proteus, who hopscotches between one love interest to another, attempts to rape Silvia, and stabs his best friend in the back.

But wait! It's possible that Eglamour is a coward. Critic Anne Barton points out that "Sir Eglamour, the romantic knight faithful unto death, abruptly turns coward and abandons Silvia to her fate when they meet the outlaws in the forest (*The Riverside Shakespeare*, 179). Hmm. Come to think of it, Barton may be right. After the outlaws capture Julia, the Third Outlaw notes that Eglamour, "being nimble-footed [...] hath outrun" them (5.3.1). In other words, when the

outlaws chased Eglamour and Silvia, Eglamour hightailed it out of there and left Silvia behind.

Antonio Character Analysis

Antonio is a Veronese nobleman and the father of Proteus. In the play, he decides to send his son to travel abroad (to Milan) so that Proteus will have a well-rounded education:

I have consider'd well his loss of time
And how he cannot be a perfect man,
Not being tried and tutor'd in the world (1.3.3)

Antonio gives voice to a pretty common Renaissance belief – that a man's education is incomplete (thereby making the man incomplete or "[im]perfect") if he doesn't venture out to see the world.

This, sadly, is the last we see of Antonio, which is too bad because we'd really like to know what Antonio would have to say about whether or not his son learns anything while he's off being "tutor'd in the world."

Character Roles

Protagonist
Proteus and Valentine's Friendship
If we think of the play as a "celebration" of male friendship, then we can also think of Proteus and Valentine's bromance as the play's major "protagonist." The relationship is put to the test by Proteus's disloyal behavior and the guys' romantic relationships with women. In the end, male friendship wins out when Valentine forgives Proteus for trying to steal his girl.

Antagonist
Proteus
When Proteus falls in love with Silvia, he decides that he's got to have her, even though his best friend is in love with her. His willingness to lie to his best bud and his relentless pursuit of Silvia (including his attempt to rape her) are major threats to the friendship.

Antagonist
Romance
If we think of male friendship as the play's "protagonist," then it sort of follows that romance acts as an antagonist to that relationship. Proteus's love for Julia causes Proteus and Valentine to be separated (Proteus stays behind in Verona instead of travelling with his pal). Proteus and Valentine also fall for the same girl, Silvia, who comes between them. Is it *fair* to blame Silvia for

Valentine and Proteus's problems? Absolutely not, but the play suggests that romantic relationships with women have the potential to breakup male friendships.

Protagonist

Romance

What? You don't like what we've argued so far? Fine. How about this – what if we argue that romance, not male friendship, is the play's "protagonist"? If we think of it this way, then it is male-female love that must overcome all obstacles. Why else, one could argue, would the play end in the promise of a double wedding?

Antagonist

Proteus

OK, if romance is the protagonist you're rooting for, then you're probably thinking Proteus is a major "antagonist," right? He's the one, after all, who chases after Silvia when she's dating his best friend and tries to rape her. This could definitely work because he's one of the major obstacles in the way of Valentine and Silvia's hook-up.

Antagonist

The Duke of Milan

The Duke of Milan is another "antagonist" to romance, don't you think? He *is* the guy who banishes Valentine from Milan and prevents him from physically being with Silvia, no?

Guide/Mentor

Lucetta (to Julia)

Lucetta is Julia's levelheaded servant. She dishes out solid advice and helps Julia cross-dress so she can track down her boyfriend in Milan. Hmm. Sounds like a "mentor" to us, even if she does have to put up with Julia's occasional tantrums.

Foil

Lance to Proteus

When Lance tells us about all the beatings he's taken for his dog Crab's bad behavior (stealing pudding, killing geese, "a pissing" under the Duke's table, etc.), it becomes pretty clear that he's more devoted to his dog than Proteus is loyal to Julia and Valentine (4.4.1). Read more about this by going to our "Characters" section.

Character Clues

Names

In Greek mythology, Proteus is a sea god who changes his shape at will. So, it seems pretty fitting that Shakespeare's fickle character, Proteus, shares the same name because the guy falls in and out of love like some people change outfits. Proteus is also pretty good at disguising his true intentions so we could also say that his lies and deceit also make him a kind of immoral

shape-shifter.

Valentine shares his name with St. Valentine, the patron saint of lovers. This seems ironic in the first scene because Valentine hates on love and makes fun of Proteus for being into Julia. The name begins to make more sense when Valentine falls for Silvia and hatches a plan to run away with her.

The name "Crab" belongs to Lance's surly natured dog, so it might be a reference to "crab apples," which are kind of sour.

Love and Romance
Ever notice the way Valentine talks about romance? It's always in an elevated, over-the-top way. In a monologue about his girlfriend, Valentine asks "What light is light if Silvia be not seen?/ What joy is joy, if Silvia be not by?" (3.1.15). Pretty poetic, wouldn't you say? We might also say that this is a little *too* over the top. Valentine elevates Silvia in an unrealistic way so we might question whether or not his love is genuine, especially since he basically offers her to Proteus in the final scene.

In contrast, when Lance falls in love with a girl, he explains that "She hath more qualities than a water-spaniel," before ticking off a laundry list of reasons why his new sweetie is so great: "She can fetch and carry. Why, a horse/ can do no more: nay, a horse cannot fetch, but only/ carry; therefore is she better than a jade." Plus, he says, "She can milk" a cow (3.1.6). Lance's ideas about love are practical – he's obviously interested in qualities that would make for a good wife, which, in Lance's mind, seems to be nothing more than a servant.

Literary Devices

Symbols, Imagery, Allegory

Nightingales
When Valentine gets kicked out of Milan for trying to elope with the Duke's daughter, he bums around a forest, where he finds a sense of peace bemoaning his sadness in harmony with the mournful sounds of the nightingale:

This shadowy desert, unfrequented woods,
I better brook than flourishing peopled towns:
Here can I sit alone, unseen of any,
And to the nightingale's complaining notes
Tune my distresses and record my woes. (5.4.1)

What's all this nightingale stuff about, you ask? Well, on the one hand, Valentine's reference

to the bird's sad music reminds of an earlier moment when he said that, without his beloved Silvia, "There is no music in the nightingale" (3.1.15). OK, we get it. Valentine is sad and lonely without his girlfriend. So much so that not even the otherwise cheerful sound of birdsong can make him happy.

There's also another meaning in Valentine's "nightingale" reference. As literary scholar Jean Howard reminds us, this passage *also* recalls the mythic story of Philomela, who was raped by Tereus and eventually transformed into a nightingale whose sad tune mourned the loss of Philomela's virginity. (You can read all about Philomela and Tereus in our summary of Ovid's *Metamorphoses*, Book 6.)

OK, we know what you're thinking. What does the mythic story of Philomela's rape and transformation into a bird have to do with Valentine hanging out in the forest missing his girlfriend? Well, it can't be a coincidence that moments after Valentine mentions the nightingale, his pal Proteus tries to rape Silvia in the very same forest, can it? We know of course that Proteus doesn't succeed (Valentine stops him) but the potential for sexual violence is still there.

In fact, the threat of rape echoes all over the play. It's the reason why Julia disguises herself as "Sebastian" – so she can avoid "loose encounters of lascivious men" (2.7.4). When Valentine makes the outlaws swear to "do no outrages/ On silly women" (4.1.12), it becomes evident that rape is a real possibility for women travelling through the forest. So, it seems like the mournful "nightingale" can function as a symbol of the potential for sexual assault in the play.

Crab the Dog

Crab is Lance's beloved dog. According to Lance, Crab also happens to be an ungrateful little cur. When Lance announces to his family that his job as Proteus's servant is taking him away from home to the Duke's court of Milan, his family is devastated. The dog? Not so much.

I think Crab, my dog, be the sourest-natured
dog that lives: my mother weeping, my father
wailing, my sister crying, our maid howling, our cat
wringing her hands, and all our house in a great
perplexity, yet did not this cruel-hearted cur shed
one tear: he is a stone, a very pebble stone, and
has no more pity in him than a dog: (2.3.1)

Lance's relationship with his dog seems like a parody of the romantic relationships between the play's couples, don't you think? Crab, like Proteus, is loved and adored but he's not very loyal. (Dogs are *supposed* to be sad when their masters' leave. Just ask Argos, Odysseus' faithful hound in the *Odyssey*.) Lance, on the other hand, is loyal to a fault. (Kind of like Julia. We could also compare Lance and Crab to Proteus and Valentine.) In fact, Lance even takes the blame when Crab gets caught "a pissing" under the table at the Duke's place (4.4.1).

Lance's reward for his devotion to his pooch? Not so much as slobbery kiss from Crab. Instead, Lance takes a beating for supposedly wetting his pants. Ah, the things we do for love.

Fun Fact: In the film *Shakespeare in Love*, Queen Elizabeth I's favorite part of *Two Gentlemen of Verona* is the "bit with the dog." Go to "Best of the Web" videos for a link to a great clip from the film.

Rings

Gosh. It seems like there's a lot of finger bling in this play. Julia and Proteus exchange rings in Act 2, Scene 3, Proteus asks Sebastian to deliver a ring to Silvia in Act 4, Scene 4, and then in Act 5, Scene 4 "Sebastian" gives Proteus the ring that he, Proteus, originally gave to Julia (back in Act 2). Then, "Sebastian" brags to Proteus that "Julia" gave it to him (5.4). Are you dizzy yet?

Here's the thing. There are only two rings in the play – the ones Julia and Proteus first exchanged when they said goodbye to each other (2.3). These two rings then get circulated to other characters, which means that Proteus gives (or tries to give) Silvia the very *same* ring that Julia gave him. (Nice guy, huh?)

Silvia, however, doesn't want Proteus's gift. Here's what she has to say when she realizes Proteus is trying to give her Julia's ring:

The more shame for him that he sends it me;
For I have heard him say a thousand times
His Julia gave it him at his departure.
Though his false finger have profaned the ring,
Mine shall not do his Julia so much wrong. (4.4.4)

Ordinarily, rings are supposed to be symbolic of a couple's love and commitment, right? Well, this isn't necessarily the case in *Two Gentleman of Verona*. We could argue that, by the time Julia's ring reaches Silvia, it has become emblematic of Proteus's deception and his broken promises. On the other hand, we can also argue that Silvia's rejection of the ring (on the grounds that accepting it from a loser like Proteus would hurt Julia and Valentine) is symbolic of her loyalty to Valentine and her sense of allegiance toward another woman.

The Forest

When Valentine gets booted out of Milan for trying to elope with Silvia, he flees to a forest somewhere between Milan and Mantua, where he quickly becomes the leader of a band of outlaws (who have also been banished from court). Although Valentine misses Silvia and thinks that keeping his crew of thieving outlaws out of trouble is hard work, things are hunky dory in the forest. He says so himself: "How use doth breed a habit in a man!/ This shadowy desert, unfrequented woods,/ I better brook than flourishing peopled towns" (5.4.1). In other words, Valentine could get used to the simple life. In the forest, he doesn't have to worry about the chaos of court or the problems that come with his romantic interests.

Eventually, all of the major characters wind up here as well and the problems that follow them are quickly resolved. The Duke gives Valentine permission to marry Silvia, the outlaws are pardoned by the Duke, Proteus falls back in love with Julia, Valentine and Proteus become best buds again, and so on.

What is this? A *magic* forest? Sort of. Here's what literary critic Jean Howard has to say: "The utopian possibilities for social renewal in a world beyond the walls and customs of the city are celebrated in this play as they are later to be in *A Midsummer Night's Dream* , *As You Like It*, and other Shakespearean romantic comedies of the 1590s" (Introduction to *Two Gentlemen of Verona*, The Norton Shakespeare, 2008). In other words, the forest is a space where characters can escape from their problems and repair the social relationships that they've managed to screw up. Shakespeare really likes this convention – he's always sending his characters on vacations into the woods or the countryside where life is simpler and the air is cleaner.

For women, however, the forest is also a place of potential danger. This is where Silvia is nearly raped by Proteus (5.4) and it's also where Valentine makes his band of thieving brothers promise not to hurt any women (4.1.12), which sort of implies that women get hurt in the forest all the time. Eventually, however, the forest is where Julia's relationship with Proteus is mended and where Silvia is engaged to her sweetie, Valentine. This, by the way, is Shakespeare's way of "restoring social order" for the ladies – by hitching them to husbands.

Letters

The characters in *Two Gentlemen of Verona* pass more notes than a class full of sixth graders. They also pass more letters than in any other Shakespeare comedy. So, what's the deal with all the letters in *Two Gentlemen*? Well, the first thing to notice is that writing and passing love letters is a major component in the process of wooing (a.k.a. flirting with the intent to marry). In the play, if you want a relationship with someone, you whip up a little note that says something like "I like you. Do you like me? Mark one box – yes or no." Or if you're Silvia, you trick Valentine into writing a love letter to a "friend" so you don't seem too forward or "improper." In other words, letters are the things that help give romantic relationships a nudge in the right direction.

At the same time, however, if a steamy love note falls into the wrong hands (like when the Duke of Milan reads Valentine's letter to Silvia), a simple thing like a letter can shift the plot in an entirely new direction. In the case of the Duke reading Valentine's letter, the result is that Valentine and Silvia's plans to elope are foiled and Valentine is banished. (That's so much worse than your teacher reading your note aloud to the class, isn't it?)

Setting

Verona, Duke's Court in Milan, a Forest between Milan and Mantua
Verona to Milan

The setting of *Two Gentlemen* can be a bit confusing because, in the 1623 folio edition (the only early copy of the play we have), there are several inconsistencies about geographic location. Here's what you need to remember: the play begins in Verona (Valentine and Proteus's home town) and then moves to the Duke's court in Milan. Then most of the cast travels to a forest (somewhere between Milan and Mantua).

The Duke's court in Milan is portrayed as a worldly, cosmopolitan kind of place. This, after all, is where the fathers of Proteus and Valentine send their sons to learn a thing or two about the great big "world." This becomes clear when Panthino advises Antonio:

Twere good, I think, your lordship sent him thither:
There shall he practise tilts and tournaments,
Hear sweet discourse, converse with noblemen.
And be in eye of every exercise
Worthy his youth and nobleness of birth. (1.3.4)

The Forest

We talk about the forest in "Symbols," but we've got to mention it here as well because it's pretty important. When Valentine gets booted out of Milan for trying to elope with Silvia, he flees to a forest somewhere between Milan and Mantua, where he quickly becomes the leader of a band of outlaws (who have also been banished from court). Although Valentine misses Silvia and thinks that keeping his crew of thieving outlaws out of trouble is hard work, things are hunky dory in the forest. He says so himself: "How use doth breed a habit in a man!/ This shadowy desert, unfrequented woods,/ I better brook than flourishing peopled towns" (5.4.1). In other words, Valentine could get used to the simple life. In the forest, he doesn't have to worry about the chaos of court or the problems that come with his romantic interests.

Eventually, all of the major characters wind up here as well and the problems that follow them are quickly resolved. The Duke gives Valentine permission to marry Silvia, the outlaws are pardoned by the Duke, Proteus falls back in love with Julia, Valentine and Proteus become best buds again, and so on.

What is this? A *magic* forest? Sort of. Here's what literary critic Jean Howard has to say: "The utopian possibilities for social renewal in a world beyond the walls and customs of the city are celebrated in this play as they are later to be in *A Midsummer Night's Dream* , *As You Like It*, and other Shakespearean romantic comedies of the 1590s" (Introduction to *Two Gentlemen of Verona*, The Norton Shakespeare, 2008). In other words, the forest is a space where characters can escape from their problems and repair the social relationships that they've managed to screw up. Shakespeare really likes this convention – he's always sending his characters on vacations into the woods or the countryside, where life is simpler and the air is cleaner.

For women, however, the forest is also a place of potential danger. This is where Silvia is nearly raped by Proteus (5.4) and it's also where Valentine makes his band of thieving brothers promise not to hurt any women (4.1.12), which sort of implies that women get hurt in the forest all the time. Eventually, however, the forest is where Julia's relationship with Proteus is mended and where Silvia is engaged to her sweetie, Valentine. This, by the way, is Shakespeare's way of "restoring social order" for the ladies – by hitching them to husbands.

Genre

Comedy

We've said this before but it's important to say it again here – as Shakespeare's very first "comedy" (probably his very first play), *Two Gentlemen of Verona* is a template for all of the Shakespearean comedies that follow. So, it seems like a good idea to come up with a nifty list of conventions that Shakespeare sticks with throughout his career.

Comedy Checklist

- **Light, Humorous Tone:** Check. For the most part, *Two Gentlemen of Verona* is pretty humorous in tone. Although it explores some pretty weighty issues – like sex, violence, and love – it does so with a fairly light and irreverent hand. Take, for example, the way Shakespeare parodies conventional ideas about love and loyalty by creating a character (Lance) that is more loyal and devoted to his dog "Crab" than some of the main characters are devoted to their romantic partners and friends. (Proteus, we're talking about you here.)

  That said, *Two Gentlemen* also has some pretty dark undertones. For the play's female characters, sexual assault is a constant threat – after all, it's the reason why Julia disguises herself as a boy page while she travels to Milan. As we know, Proteus nearly rapes Silvia in Act 5, Scene 4, until his assault is thwarted by Valentine.

- **Clever Dialogue and Witty Banter:** Check. Although, literary critic Harold Goddard once wrote that *Two Gentlemen* "contains some of the most boring wit," we'd like to point out a couple of things. First, Speed has a penchant for clever puns and fast wit. Second, witty repartee is a major component of the flirting ("wooing" if you live in the sixteenth century) that goes on in this play. So, while the dialogue may not be as great as the snappy banter in, say, *The Taming of the Shrew*, it's still pretty darn clever.

- **Deception and Disguise:** Check. Proteus is responsible for most of the deception in the play. He sneakily betrays Julia and Valentine when he makes a play for Silvia and he lies to the Duke and Thurio. Julia and Silvia, to some extent, are also guilty of deception insofar

as they tend to play mind games with their suitors at the beginning of the play. Of course, Julia pulls off the ultimate disguise, which you can read about below.

- **Mistaken Identity:** Check. When Julia cross-dresses as "Sebastian," her cheating boyfriend, Proteus, doesn't recognize her. In fact, he hires "Sebastian" as his page boy and sends "him" on an errand to deliver a ring (the same ring Julia gave Proteus at the beginning of the play) to Silvia.

- **Love Overcomes Obstacles:** Check. Julia and Proteus's romantic relationship survives Julia's silly mind games, Proteus's journey to Milan, and astonishingly, Proteus's attempted rape of Silvia. Similarly, Valentine and Silvia manage to get together (*with* the Duke's approval) despite the following hurdles: the Duke's banishment of Valentine from Milan, the Duke's plans for Silvia to wed Thurio, and, again, Proteus's attempted rape of Silvia.

- **Family Drama:** Check. Proteus is mad at his dad for sending him to Milan when all he wants to do is hang out with Julia. The Duke treats his daughter like a piece of property that he can bestow on any man of his choosing (Thurio and then Valentine when Thurio turns out to be a loser). Julia runs away from home, and so on. But don't worry because things *always* work out for families in plays like this, so keep reading....

- **Multiple Plots with Twists and Turns:** Check. This one is pretty self-explanatory, especially if you've been paying attention to what we've been saying.

- **(Re) unification of Families:** Check. Cover your eyes if you don't want us to ruin the ending.... In the play's last scene, Silvia's dad (the Duke) shows up and says it's OK for Valentine and Silvia to get hitched. Hooray! We're so glad *Two Gentlemen* is a "comedy" and not a "tragedy," because now Silvia and Valentine don't have to pull a "Romeo and Juliet" (secretly elope and then, well, you know what happens at the end of *that* play). Although he never speaks to his daughter directly (what's up with that?), we can assume he's forgiven her for running off into the forest. So, with Silvia, the Duke, and Silvia's soon-to-be-husband on good terms, we've got ourselves a little family reunion.

- **Marriage:** Check. Check. Shakespeare's comedies always, always, always end with a marriage (or the promise of one). In this play's final lines, Valentine turns to his buddy Proteus (who has just gotten re-engaged to Julia), and says "our day of marriage shall be yours,/ one feast, one house, one mutual happiness" (5.4.14). In other words, both couples

are getting hitched in a double wedding back at the Duke's place.

More to Explore...

OK, now you know why we categorize *Two Gentlemen of Verona* as a "comedy." But don't just take our word for it. Compare this list to our discussions of "Genre" in some of Shakespeare's others comedies, like, say, *Twelfth Night*. You might also want to think about how "comedy" is different than "tragedy." (We've got a handy checklist for that too. See, for example, our discussion of *Hamlet's* genre.

Writing Style

Verse and Prose

Reading any one of Shakespeare's plays can feel like reading a really lengthy poem and that's because they're written in a combination of verse (poetry) and prose (how we talk every day). We break all of this down in the paragraphs that follow but here's what you should remember about Shakespeare's plays, *Two Gentlemen* included: the nobility tend to speak in verse, which is a pretty formal way to talk. The commoners, or "Everyday Joes" tend to speak just like we do, in regular prose. (Note: The play *Richard II* is the *one* exception to this rule – it's the only Shakespeare play written *entirely* in verse – even the gardeners speak poetry.)

Iambic Pentameter (The Nobles)

In *Two Gentlemen of Verona*, the noble characters typically speak in iambic pentameter. (However, since this is likely Shakespeare's very first play, a lot of the meter tends to be pretty irregular.) Don't let the fancy name intimidate you – it's really pretty simple once you get the hang of it.

An "iamb" is an unaccented syllable followed by an accented one. "Penta" means "five," and "meter" refers to a regular rhythmic pattern. So "iambic pentameter" is a kind of *rhythmic pattern* that consist of *five iambs* per line. It's the most common rhythm in English poetry and sounds like five heartbeats:

ba-DUM, ba-DUM, ba-DUM, ba-DUM, ba-DUM

Let's try it out on this line, where Julia screams at her serving woman:

what FOOL is SHE that KNOWS i AM a MAID

Every second syllable is accented (stressed) so this is classic iambic pentameter.

Prose

The servants, like Speed and Lance, speak in prose, just like we talk every day. Prose is less formal than verse, so it's befitting of the servants' social status. Here's an example, where Lance tells the audience about how his dog peed under the Duke's table:

He thrusts me himself into the company of three or four
gentlemanlike dogs under the duke's table: he had
not been there--bless the mark!--a pissing while, but
all the chamber smelt him. 'Out with the dog!' says
one: 'What cur is that?' says another: 'Whip him
out' says the third: 'Hang him up' says the Duke.   (4.4.1)

Lance's speech isn't fancy but it sure is entertaining.

What's Up With the Ending?

"All that was mine in Silvia I give thee"

The ending of *Two Gentlemen of Verona* is one of the most bizarre and disturbing endings that we've ever read. After Valentine puts a stop to Proteus's attempted rape of Silvia, Valentine does something obnoxious – he yells at Proteus for being a lousy friend but says nothing about Proteus's violation of Silvia. Proteus apologizes immediately and then, in a gesture of good will, Valentine says, "All that was mine in Silvia I give thee" (5.4.5).

Most critics interpret this line to mean that Valentine is offering to "give" Silvia to his friend as a peace offering that will secure Valentine's friendship with Proteus. Read this way, the play would seem to champion male friendship above all other relationships – especially heterosexual romance. This is certainly what happens in one of Shakespeare's major sources for *Two Gentlemen*. In the story of Titus and Gisippus (related first by Boccaccio and later retold in Thomas Elyot's 1531 *Book of the Governor*), Gisippus gives his best friend, Titus, the woman he is supposed to marry after Titus falls in love with her (*Book Named the Governor, 2.12*).

Some critics, however, have been known to read the lines a bit differently – they argue that Shakespeare is trying to reconcile the tension between male friendship and male-female romance. For these critics, Valentine means to say something like "all the love I feel for Silvia, I give to thee, too." In other words, Valentine could be saying that he will love his friend and girlfriend equally.

For some other critics, the ending is just too terrible – from a moral perspective and also from an artistic standpoint. Anne Barton writes that "the play's resolution is achieved through a movement of plot so brusque, so destructive of the relationships of the characters as they have been developed, that generations of commentators have tried to absolve Shakespeare from

Valentine's overgenerous gift of his lady Silvia to his friend Proteus, the man who had been doing his best to rape her only a moment before" (*The Riverside Shakespeare* 177).

The Double Wedding Promise

As disturbing as the ending is, in some ways, the play's final scene is predictable. That's because Shakespearean comedies *always* end with marriage (or the promise of one).

So, we're not completely shocked when Silvia's dad (the Duke) shows up and says it's OK for Valentine and Silvia to get hitched. We are, however, baffled when Julia takes Proteus back after she watches him try to rape Silvia. Even so, we're left with the promise of a double wedding when, in the play's final lines, Valentine turns to Proteus and says, "our day of marriage shall be yours,/ one feast, one house, one mutual happiness" (5.4.14). Does this mean that Valentine's bromance with Proteus is being replaced by his marriage to Silvia? Not necessarily.

Valentine's "one mutual happiness" comment is ambiguous. On the one hand, it seems to be a play on the biblical idea that, when a man and woman marry, they become united as "one flesh" (Genesis 2.24). If this is the case, then Valentine could be referring to the "mutual happiness" shared between a bride and groom. The funny thing is, Valentine isn't talking to his future wife here. He's speaking *to Proteus*. This makes us wonder if the "one mutual happiness" comment is an echo of the idea that male friendship turns men into two halves of the same person. In Book 2 of Thomas Elyot's *The Book Named the Governor* (a major literary influence on Shakespeare's play), Elyot writes that male bonds are a "blessed and stable connection of sundry wills, *making of two persons one* in having and suffering" (emphasis ours). The idea that Valentine and Proteus are two halves of the same person is an idea that appears more than once in the play and we talk about this in "Quotes" for "Friendship." So, is Valentine suggesting that he and Proteus will share "one mutual happiness"? Something else?

These final lines are pretty tricky. How we interpret them is likely to determine how we interpret the entire play – does Valentine's final speech resolve all of the tension between male friendship and male-female romance that we've seen throughout the play? Or does it verify that male friendship is more important than everything else?

Did You Know?

Trivia

- *Two Gentlemen of Verona* is very likely Shakespeare's first play. (source: Jean E. Howard, Introduction to the Norton Shakespeare edition of *Two Gentlemen of Verona*, 2008)

- If *Two Gentlemen* is Shakespeare's very first play, then it follows that "Julia" is Shakespeare's very first cross-dressing heroine.

- The 1998 film *Shakespeare in Love* uses speeches, scenes, themes, and the "bit with the dog" from *Two Gentlemen of Verona*, including Valentine's big "What light is light, if Silvia be not seen?" speech in Act 3, Scene 1. Check out this clip from the film. About four minutes in, a cross-dressed Viola (Gwyneth Paltrow) auditions for Will Shakespeare's (Joseph Fiennes) new play and recites Valentine's lines from *Two Gentlemen of Verona.*

- In July 2007, BBC radio aired *Two Gentlemen of Valasna,* an adaptation set in mid-seventeenth-century India "in the weeks leading up to the Indian Mutiny of 1857." (source)

- Soon after the release of the 2009 film *I Love You Man Time* magazine came out with a list of the "Top Ten Movie Bromances." We *can't* believe *Two Gentlemen of Verona* didn't make it. (source)

- In 1971, *Two Gentlemen of Verona* was adapted into a Tony Award winning rock musical featuring songs like "Love Drove Me Sane" and "Don't Have the Baby." (source)

- *Two Gentlemen of Verona* features the smallest cast of any Shakespeare play. (source: Jean E. Howard, Introduction to the Norton Shakespeare edition of *Two Gentlemen of Verona*, 2008)

Steaminess Rating

R
We're giving this play an "R" rating because Proteus comes pretty close to raping Silvia in Act 5, Scene 4. In fact, the threat of rape is a running theme throughout the play, which you can read more about by going to our discussion of the theme of "Violence."

Allusions and Cultural References

Literary Sources

- Jorge de Montemay, or *Diana Enamorada* (published in English 1598)
- Anonymous, *The History of Felix and Philomela* (a lost play)
- Thomas Elyot, Book 2, Chapter 12 of *The Book Named the Governor* (1531)

Major Literary Influences

- John Lyly, *Euphues, the Anatomy of Wit* (1578)
- Arthur Brookes, *The Tragicall History of Romeus and Juliet* (1562)

Mythology, Legends, and Biblical Allusions

- The character Proteus shares his name with the shape-shifting sea god.
- The character Valentine shares his name with the patron saint of lovers.
- Myth of Hero and Leander (1.1)
- Cupid (2.4)
- Greek myth of Phaëton, who set the world on fire driving his dad's chariot (3.1)
- The Temptation of Eve in the Garden of Eden (3.1)
- Greek myth of Ariadne, who killed herself when Theseus broke up with her (4.4)
- Greek myth of Tereus's rape of Philomela (5.4)

Best of the Web

Websites

Read the Play Online
http://shakespeare.mit.edu/two_gentlemen/
What? You left your copy of the play in your locker? Read it online, compliments of MIT.

Folger Shakespeare Library
http://www.folger.edu

This is one of the greatest Shakespeare resources around.

Movie or TV Productions

1983 BBC TV Production
http://www.imdb.com/title/tt0086492/
The film features lots of great period music and a stunning Italian setting. It's also likely to be the version your teacher shows in class.

Shakespeare in Love, 1998
http://www.imdb.com/title/tt0138097/
This movie borrows a whole lot from *Two Gentlemen of Verona* and it's a must see for anyone who has read the play or just loves Shakespeare.

"Two Gentlemen of Capeside" (*Dawson's Creek*)
http://www.twiztv.com/scripts/dawsonscreek/season4/dawson-403.htm
If you're into *Dawson's Creek* reruns, then you might remember how best buds Dawson and Pacey fought over Joey (Katie Holmes) in Season 4. "Two Gentlemen of Capeside" is a loose adaptation of Shakespeare's play, which Dawson and Joey are studying at the beginning of the episode. You can read the script here.

A Spray of Plum Blossoms (Yi jian mei), 1931
http://www.imdb.com/title/tt0192842/
This silent Chinese film is considered a loose adaptation of *Two Gentlemen of Verona.*

Love Shakespeare and German Language? This is the flick for you.
http://www.imdb.com/title/tt0131150/
Zwei Herren aus Verona ("Two Gentlemen of Verona") is a 1964 TV production of the play.

Historical Documents

First Folio Edition of Two Gentlemen of Verona (1623)
http://files.libertyfund.org/files/1112/02Verona_Bk.pdf
Read the first published version of the play – The Online Library of Liberty has made it available as an image-based PDF file.

Video

Valentine's "What light is light" Speech
http://www.youtube.com/watch?v=D2XVFcfEhAk&feature=related
This clip from *Shakespeare in Love* features Viola (played by Gwyneth Paltrow) cross-dressing as a boy to audition for Shakespeare's new play. She recites Valentine's famous "What light is light, if Silvia be not seen?" speech from Act 3, Scene 1 of *Two Gentlemen of Verona.* The speech begins about three and a half minutes into this clip.

Two Gentlemen Go To...Broadway
http://www.youtube.com/watch?v=3k9WtCDnyB8&feature=related
Watch a clip from a musical adaptation of Shakespeare's *Two Gentlemen of Verona.*

Doggie Auditions for the Part of "Crab"
http://www.youtube.com/watch?v=-nuSGHS7_tA
We don't know if Shakespeare used a real dog to play the part of "Crab" on stage, but most modern productions of the play use a live animal. Check out this clip, where dogs audition for the Colorado Shakespeare Festival's production of *Two Gentlemen.*

Audio
Got Two Minutes?
http://www.learnoutloud.com/Catalog/Arts-and-Entertainment/Full-Cast-Dramatization/Two-Gentlemen-of-Verona/15070
Listen to Speed and Proteus argue about whether or not Speed is a "sheep" (1.1). (Hint: click "Hear Sample.")

"Would Life Be Better if We All Spoke Shakespeare?"
http://www.npr.org/templates/story/story.php?storyId=9849018
Listen to this NPR podcast about how we incorporate Shakespeare into our everyday conversations without even knowing it. Includes an interview with one of our very favorite scholars, Gail Kern Paster.

Images
Great Artwork Inspired By the Play
http://shakespeare.emory.edu/illustrated_playdisplay.cfm?playid=33
Check out some of the artwork (with commentary) inspired by *Two Gentlemen.*

Proteus and Valentine
http://upload.wikimedia.org/wikipedia/commons/4/44/Valentine_and_Proteus.jpg
This image captures Proteus and Valentine's reluctant goodbye in Act 1, Scene 1.

Salvador Dali's *Two Gentlemen of Verona*
http://rogallery.com/Dali_Salvador/w-366/Dali-Two%20Gentlemen%20of%20Verona.htm
Dali completed several Shakespeare inspired etchings (c. 1971).

"Lance's Substitute for Proteus's Dog" (1849)
http://shakespeare.emory.edu/illustrated_showimage.cfm?imageid=63
This oil painting is on display at the Leicestershire Museum and Art Gallery.

16330706R00050

Printed in Great Britain
by Amazon